PERGAMON INTERNATIONAL LIBRARY
of Science, Technology, Engineering and Social Studies

*The 1000-volume original paperback library in aid of education,
industrial training and the enjoyment of leisure*

Publisher: Robert Maxwell, M.C.,

PEOPLE, COMMUNICATION AND ORGANISATION

A Case Study Approach

THE PERGAMON TEXTBOOK
INSPECTION COPY SERVICE

An inspection copy of any book published in the Pergamon International Library will
gladly be sent to academic staff without obligation for their consideration for course
adoption of recommendation. Copies may be retained for a period of 60 days from
receipt and returned if not suitable. When a particular title is adopted or recommended for adoption for class use and the recommendation results in a sale of 12 or
more copies the inspection copy may be retained with our compliments. The Publishers will be ... titles to be
published in ...

Other Titles of Interest

DUBRIN, A J
Casebook of Organizational Behavior

EILON, S
Aspects of Management

GREENER, M
Between the Lines of the Balance Sheet

IBRAHIM, I B
Readings in Managerial Economics

SASAKI, N
Management and Industrial Structure in Japan

UKTA
Exporting to the UK

Related Journal

OMEGA*

The International Journal of Management Science

Chief Editor: Samuel Eilon, Imperial College of Science and Technology,
London, UK

OMEGA provides all specialists in management science with important new
developments in operational research and managerial economics. Published
material ranges from original contributions to review articles describing the
state-of-the-art in specific areas, together with shorter critical assessments of
particular management techniques.

*Free specimen copy available on request.

PEOPLE, COMMUNICATION
AND
ORGANISATION

A Case Study Approach

by

JOSEPH CHILVER

DORSET INSTITUTE OF HIGHER EDUCATION, U.K.

PERGAMON PRESS

OXFORD · NEW YORK · TORONTO · SYDNEY · PARIS · FRANKFURT

U.K.	Pergamon Press Ltd., Headington Hill Hall, Oxford OX3 0BW, England
U.S.A.	Pergamon Press Inc., Maxwell House, Fairview Park, Elmsford, New York 10523, U.S.A.
CANADA	Pergamon Press Canada Ltd., Suite 104, 150 Consumers Road, Willowdale, Ontario M2J 1P9, Canada
AUSTRALIA	Pergamon Press (Aust.) Pty. Ltd., P.O. Box 544, Potts Point, N.S.W. 2011, Australia
FRANCE	Pergamon Press SARL, 24 rue des Ecoles, 75240 Paris, Cedex 05, France
FEDERAL REPUBLIC OF GERMANY	Pergamon Press GmbH, D–6242 Kronberg-Taunus, Hammerweg 6, Federal Republic of Germany

First edition 1984

Library of Congress Cataloging in Publication Data

Chilver, J. W. (Joseph W.)
People, communication, & organisation.
(Pergamon international library of science, technology, engineering, and social studies)
1. Management–Case studies. 2. Personnel management–Case studies. I. Title. II. Title: People, communication, and organisations. III. Series.
HD31.C477   1983   658.3   83–13282

British Library Cataloguing in Publication Data

Chilver, J. W.
People, communication and organisation. — (Pergamon international library of science, technology engineering and social studies)
1. Management   2. Decision-making
I. Title
658.4'03   HD69.4

ISBN 0–08–030838–4 (Hard cover)
ISBN 0–08–030839–2 (Flexicover)

Printed in Great Britain by A. Wheaton & Co. Ltd., Exeter

Preface

Much of the case study material herein is adapted from my earlier book
The Human Aspects of Management: A Case Study Approach. As
revised, I am hoping it will be of interest to students on a variety of
business and management courses particularly those under the auspices of
the Business Education Council and the Institute of Commercial Management.

All the case studies herein are based on personal experience directly or
indirectly obtained but the names of characters and companies have been
changed.

JOSEPH CHILVER

Acknowledgements

The authors and publishers wish to thank the undermentioned for permission to include various extracts as acknowledged in the text:

Daily Telegraph
The Observer
The Times

The author also wishes to thank Ian Mackay and Martin Deeley, his colleagues at the Dorset Institute of Higher Education, for their helpful ideas and suggestions.

Contents

III. Problems Centred on Personnel   95

IV. Problems Centred on Industrial Relations   131

Compendium   159

Guidelines   181

Index   217

SECTION I

Problems Centred on Human Relations

CASE 1

People at Work

Those who have experience of the work situation will no doubt confirm that one of the most pleasant aspects of business is meeting and talking to people. By definition, business would be impossible without people consulting and conferring with each other. And so our relationships with other people are not a peripheral concern. They are a vital dimension in the world of business in which we find ourselves. What sort of people are you likely to meet in a typical working day? Here is a selection of your probable contacts:

(a) Your own manager (or supervisor) — possibly higher ranking managers.
(b) Colleagues and workmates at the same level in the hierarchy (these are often described as your "peers").
(c) Those for whom you are responsible — the word "subordinate" is often used though some people object to it.
(d) Customers and potential customers seeking information, assistance and possibly advice.
(e) Solicitors and accountants and all sorts of professionals and people associated with them.

It follows that there are advantages to be gained in learning to cope with other people in our business lives. If we could understand people a little better we might be able to deal with the problems they pose more effectively. There are two vital questions for us to consider:

1. Why do people behave as they do?
2. What can we do to get the best out of our relationships with other people both for the benefit of our employer and for our own benefit?

Although these questions may seem difficult to answer, we do have a certain amount of evidence at our disposal and an attempt will now be made to integrate some of the research in the hope that it will help us to cope with the problem situations posed in the case studies which follow.

Motivation

The first point to note is that without motivation people are inanimate objects. There has to be an explanation for everything we do. At the lowest level we could be described as pleasure-seeking/pain-avoiding animals, but human behaviour is obviously more complex than that. Perhaps we are constantly striving to satisfy an endless assortment of needs. This is certainly how the American psychologist, *Abraham Maslow*, saw the problem. Of course we have needs and try to satisfy them, but according to Maslow the needs are not random and unstructured. He saw our needs taking the form of a pyramid or hierarchy as in Fig.1.

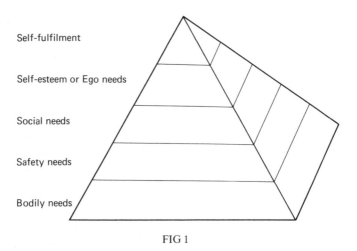

FIG 1

Maslow saw people as perpetually wanting. As one set of needs are largely satisfied, the needs at the next level become activated. At the first level in the hierarchy man is predominantly concerned with his bodily needs. His thoughts are concentrated on bread so long as he is hungry. But as soon as his hunger is appeased another set of needs is activated. Now man begins to concentrate his thoughts on his personal safety and the safety of his material possessions. These first two levels might be equated to man's economic needs. And man is not simply an economic animal. When he is largely satisfied in terms of bodily and safety needs, he begins to become concerned about the opinions of those around him. Man hungers for love, affection and respect. He becomes as hungry for approbation as he was originally hungry for food.

One of the explanations for particular behaviour can well be the individual's willingness to conform to the norms imposed by any of the groups

within which he functions from time to time. As defined by R. Dewey and
W. Humber:*

> "Norms are explicit or implicit statements defining what
> behaviour is desirable, necessary and encouraged or undesir-
> able, harmful and forbidden. They must be implemented by
> sanctions ranging from imprisonment through heavy fines or
> ostracism, to verbal reprimands and other forms of social or
> self-censorship. On the other hand are the rewards ranging from
> the freedom from force or coercion, through monetary gains . . .
> to simple approbation for conformity."

Be it noted that the giving or withholding of approbation (love affection
and respect) is one of the primary regulators of human behaviour which
gives strength to Maslow's proposition that our social needs occupy the
central ground in his hierarchy. Nor are the social pressures trivial. From
Dewey and Humber again:

> "Most of what the individual learns is determined by the cus-
> toms and fashions of his society. He speaks the language, eats
> the foods, wears the clothes, thinks the thoughts and accepts
> the attitudes that are prepared for him by his associates and
> ancestors."

Man's behaviour is moulded to a great extent by his environment. "Bad"
behaviour can often be explained by a "bad" environment. So if we want
to change man's behaviour we shall often need to change his environment.
Of course, part of the all-powerful environment is represented by the
people with whom the individual comes into contact. And the various
groups (see Fig.2) exercise control over the individual by giving or
withholding the approval for which he craves.

Even when man is not deprived of affection or social approval a new
want emerges. Now man becomes egocentric. He hungers for ego food:
self-assurance and self-esteem. One of the basic similarities in all human
beings is the possession of an ego. It may remain submerged for long
periods of time. Some people are more ego-sensitive than others in the
same way that some have bigger appetites, but sooner or later everyone
faces ego problems in a modern industrial society.

What is the ego? It is the highly prized Self around which we muster all
our conscious and subconscious resources of mind and body — from time
to time. The ego-less man does not exist and the extent of his ego-

*From An Introduction to Social Psychology by Collier Macmillan, London, 1966.

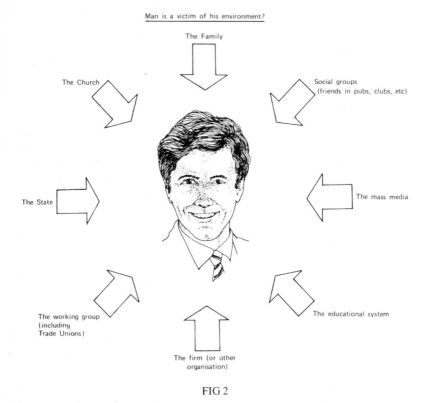

FIG 2

sensitivity can be gauged by reference to the ego defence mechanisms which are brought into play whenever the ego is threatened. For example:

   (i) *Repression* — A man conveniently forgets something that makes him subconsciously uncomfortable. A young man is driving his girl-friend home from a late night party. The car runs off the road and smashes into a tree. The last thing the young man sees before he loses consciousness is his girl-friend being hurled through the windscreen. He remembers nothing about the accident when he recovers consciousness. His mind is a complete blank in relation to the accident and his amnesia has allowed him to preserve his ego. Such is the sensitivity of the human mind we are dealing with in the business world — or elsewhere.

  (ii) *Displacement* — The boss admonishes me and I cannot retaliate without losing my job. It is an ego-bruising situation. But when I get home my wife is waiting for me and I can vent my wrath on her. Or, if she is a dominant character, I can "take it out" on the

children — or the dog. This can be described as "scapegoating".
We preserve our own egos by attacking someone else.

(iii) *Rationalisation* — Subconsciously an individual knows he is behav-
ing badly but to admit it to himself would damage his ego, so he
finds an excuse. The student who misses lectures because he is lazy
"decides" that the lectures are boring — or that the subject is
unimportant.

Using these defence mechanisms help us to protect ourselves from
psychological battering but the underlying problems remain. What needs
to be understood by the student of human behaviour attempting to apply
this knowledge to real-life business situations is that the people we are
dealing with are highly sensitive. The thwarting of our ego needs can lead
to basic discouragement — and, in extreme cases, suicide.

According to Maslow, even when our need for self-esteem is largely
satisfied it only leads to another type of need being activated — the need
for self-fulfilment. This is the desire of an individual to achieve all that he is
capable of achieving. It is associated with personal growth.

Maslow's Key Contribution

One could argue forever about the universal validity or otherwise of
Maslow's theory. It could explain the durability of a religion such as
Christianity which deals with human needs at every level in the hierarchy.
It could also be used to account for the "more and ever more" philosophy
in trade union bargaining. It certainly illustrates the dilemma facing the
businessman who strives to motivate his workteam by "catering for their
needs". An excellent aim — but difficult to achieve when satisfying one
need simply leads to the activation of another!

However, Maslow's conclusion is not controversial. By our own observa-
tions it becomes obvious that man is never satisfied. He is by nature "a
perpetually wanting animal".

Frustration Instigated Behaviour

According to the Concise Oxford Dictionary, being frustrated is "being
discontented through an inability to achieve one's desires". This seems to
suggest that "a perpetually wanting animal could also be described as a
perpetually *frustrated* animal, which brings us to a consideration of
research undertaken by one of Maslow's compatriots, Norman Maier. Rats
were used in the experiments, being placed in cages and faced with two
distinctive doors. Behind the one was a reward in the form of food. The
other door provided a punishment in the form of a fall into a net. Initially

the rats were allowed to choose between the doors in a rational fashion, but subsequently electrified grids were inserted and a random pattern of rewards and punishments were introduced. The rats were forced to make choices between the doors but no longer were their choices rational.

Maier found that both in rats and humans frustration often leads to aggressive behaviour. People who become angry become irrational and display various physical symptoms. Their pupils become dilated. The heart beats faster. Blood pressure is raised. Muscular spasms occur in the stomach and the intestines. The rage will be directed in the first place against the person or object deemed to be causing the frustration. But where it is impossible for a direct attack to be made — it may be an omnipotent boss who is causing the problem — then a scapegoat will be found. The aggression will be turned against something which is available and comparatively safe as a target — perhaps a junior clerk — or a hapless caller who makes an awkward enquiry.

One is inclined to think of aggression in physical terms, in which case most of us would deny that we are aggressive. But aggression is far more often verbal. Listen to the conversations in any canteen. How often are they critical of others? And how often do you come up against aggressive driving? And aggressive attitudes at college or your place of work?

The explanation, as far as Maier is concerned, is that the aggressors are showing one of the symptoms of frustration. There are others. There is *regression* — or childishness — typified by a loss of emotional control or hypersensitivity. There is *fixation*, whereby the same action is repeated again and again. Maier's rats banged their heads against a locked door hundreds of times without even trying the unlocked door next to it. Whereas habits are normally broken when they fail to bring satisfaction, or bring punishment instead, a fixation becomes stronger in such circumstances. Perhaps the most pathetic sign of frustration is *resignation* — or "giving up". Maier's rats could be twisted round as if they were already dead. The human being's response is to feel that nothing is of any use. There is no point in trying. One might as well let it all happen!

As a result of his researches, Maier identified two different types of behaviour which he classified as motivation-induced and frustration-instigated. The former behaviour in humans is characterised by intelligently-directed activity, but it is the frustration-instigated behaviour which is interesting when we bear in mind Maslow's basic contention that man is a perpetually wanting (and therefore frustrated) animal.

Relationships

People as well as situations might cause frustration. Any relationship between individuals calls for adjustments either in attitudes, or behaviour, or both. There is an inevitable degree of frustration. You might be able to appreciate at least some of the adjustments which are called for in the following relationships:

student–lecturer
boy-friend–girl-friend
employee–employer

There is bound to be a degree of conflict and frustration in even the healthiest relationships. Indeed, there may be conflicting desires in the same person. The conflict might be between love of leisure and ambition ("I'd love to get a qualification — but there's a good show on the television tonight. I'll start tomorrow").

People need each other. They cannot function in isolation. Social interaction necessarily involves adjustment to other people. No two people have identical traits and propensities or have had identical experiences. When faced with the need for co-operation a matching of thinking patterns is required. In the work situation frustrations are likely to be greater since they arise from the imposition of others' thought patterns and values upon the individual. Working together in a team calls for a lot of adjustments all round.

Summarizing our findings at this stage, we can say that people strive to satisfy their needs but, falling short of fulfilment, they fail to do so. Their frustrations lead to various forms of aggression which are clearly observable in ourselves and those around us.

Catharsis

There is one final series of pieces to fit into the puzzle. First, it is necessary to understand what the psychologists describe as catharsis. What would happen if you put a lidless kettle of water on the cooker, having carefully plugged up the spout? The steam would be unable to escape. There would be an explosion. In the same way, tensions build up in the individual as a result of continuing frustrations. Those tensions are released in a variety of ways including "letting off steam" in one way or another — perhaps by kicking the cat (or some other scapegoat) — perhaps during the night — in your dream sequences!

The Japanese are not unaware of the problems of frustration, nor of the remedies available. In some of their larger companies a special room has been set up where frustrated workers can hit effigies of their bosses. Having "got it off their chests" they then pass back to the factory floor via a passage along which are placed various reminders of the greatness of their firm. The vacuum created by the cathartic experience is filled with inspiring thoughts.

This might just be an amusing example of the strangeness of some people. But another American psychology professor, P. Worchel, did some research on "catharsis and the relief of hostility". He gave an intake of freshmen some frustrating experiences and then, having broken down the group into sub-groups, he gave these sub-groups varying degrees of cathartic experience. At the extremes one group were given an opportunity to talk about their frustrations, while another group had to sit quietly through a straight lecture. All the students were then given an intelligence test. He found that the students who had been allowed to experience catharsis scored higher marks.

Thus, while we may not wish to emulate the Japanese with their effigy-bashing, there is some evidence to show the wisdom of the technique, and we might consider how our own workers could find ways of experiencing catharsis. Among the alternatives are:

(i) Works councils, where workers representatives and managers might meet to exchange ideas and identify problems.
(ii) Joint consultation committees, where union representatives and shop stewards can confer.
(iii) A counselling service whereby work people can discuss their personal problems with a sympathetic counsellor. This is likely to be one of the functions of the normal Personnel Department.

Maslow/Maier/Worchel

By combining the work of the three researchers we are able to provide a brief but nevertheless useful theory explaining why man behaves as he does, in industry or elsewhere, and the theory also indicates what we might have to do to solve many of the human problems we face.

The composite theory runs thus. Man strives to satisfy a variety of needs but as one need is satisfied another emerges to take its place. Man is by his nature insatiable and is therefore evidencing symptoms of frustration. Among the most common symptoms is aggression. So while we can attempt to cater for workpeoples' needs we should also be prepared to accept that these needs can never be satisfied completely in a modern industrial society. And thus we also need to give our workpeople an opportunity to experience catharsis in one form or another.

You will no doubt be surprised to discover how often this basic understanding of human behaviour will help you to solve the problems posed in the case studies which follow.

Herzberg's Hygiene-Motivation Theory

Whereas Maslow's theory relates to human behaviour generally, the research done by Frederick Herzberg, Professor of Psychology at Case Western Reserve University in Cleveland, Ohio, concerned the behaviour of people at work. Herzberg also found people striving to satisfy their needs, but he found two distinct types of need. One set of needs he refers to as the hygiene needs, these being associated with the avoidance of pain. Under this heading he found factors such as pay and working conditions which failed to interest workpeople once they were reasonably catered for. He suggested that if you want to positively motivate people you have to ensure that the hygiene factors are not troubling them, and then you concentrate on the motivating factors. These are another distinct set of needs, including a hankering for responsibility and recognition, interesting work and opportunities for promotion and personal growth.

Herzberg's theory was first applied to a group of secretaries and personal assistants in the Registrar's Department at the Bell Telephone Corporation in the United States. Management could not understand why these carefully selected young ladies were not as efficient as they ought to be. Herzberg used a technique which has since become known as *job enrichment*. He made them responsible for dealing with the various queries from the stockholders. They were allowed to sign letters under their own names, referring to the managers only when they found themselves involved with problems where help and advice were needed. The application of job enrichment was so successful at Bell Telephone that other companies — including Imperial Chemical Industries in the U.K. — were anxious to gain the same sorts of benefits.

In essence, Herzberg showed the connection between motivation and the type of work we do. He also related these to job satisfaction and personal growth.

Workteams

Work cannot be done by individuals in isolation. There is an inevitable interaction with others. This interaction may take the form of producing goods together, trading, negotiating, planning, exercising control, or running the complex system of communications which is generally described as an office. In an industrialised economy the production team is likely to number hundreds and thousands, each member of the team being in some way dependent upon all the other members of the team. Formal relationships are of necessity established, and with these formal relationships come the organisational hierarchy and the departmentalisation of the business.

One determinant in the formation of groups is the location of the workpeople. When people work together in close proximity there will be a tendency for them to think and act like a group. A group awareness and a group identity will develop. Other stimuli to group formation are similarities of occupation and/or interests. Thus we might expect to find an affinity between chartered accountants, chemists, or departmental secretaries. Members of staff will find themselves members of different groups at different times even within the single organisation. There may be times when special issues lead to the most unlikely groupings of staff, which last only until the issue has been resolved.

Apart from the formal structures there is a complex social network and employees interact with each other constantly, seldom in a random manner, rather in habitual and patterned routines. When a member of staff joins a working team the association with the other members is not likely to end when the coffee break arrives. Conversation will range over a wide range of topics and bridges will be built between the individuals in the group. Human beings are gregarious. Their longing for approbation and respect from others, and their need for ego food can be satisfied to a substantial degree within the context of the business organisation.

The Centrality of People

The role of people in business is critical whether we are talking of top managers or rank and file workers. Bearing in mind what has been said about the frustrations experienced by human beings generally, it becomes obvious that many of the problems a businessman encounters relate to the human factors in an enterprise. Thus it becomes imperative for someone who aspires to a responsible position in business to acquire at least a basic understanding of human frailties in the same way that an engineer is expected to understand the strengths and weaknesses of metals. After all the manager achieves his results through the efforts of his workteam.

As George Thomason points out:*

> ". . . Everyone who is engaged in modern work organisations, regardless of which particular concern he may be associated with, is concerned with personnel to some extent: if he manages finance, he must still work through people; if he is engaged on direct production tasks he at least works with people. Any person in a managerial or supervisory position within the organisation is therefore in a position where he cannot escape the 'management of personnel' no matter what basic function or particular specialisation he is involved in."

*From *Textbook of Personnel Management*, Institute of Personnel Management, 3rd Edition, 1978.

Of course while all managers are by definition involved with subordinates, the Personnel Manager is a specialist whose prime concern is the
provision and maintenance of the workforce. His task has two distinct yet
inter-related facets. On the one hand there is the responsibility for staffing,
essentially ensuring that staff are available in the requisite number, with
the necessary skills, at the appropriate time and place. This could be
described as the dimension of *quantity*. To this extent his job is not
dissimilar to that of a stock controller whose function is to ensure that raw
materials are available as and when required. However, the stock controller's material is inanimate whereas people are sensitive, potentially
dynamic, and capable of growth if treated properly. This leads us to the
second facet of the Personnel Manager's task. He is responsible for the
standard of morale in the workforce and its general effectiveness. This
could be seen as the dimansion of *quality*. The composition of the task
confronting a typical Personnel Manager is indicated in Fig.3.

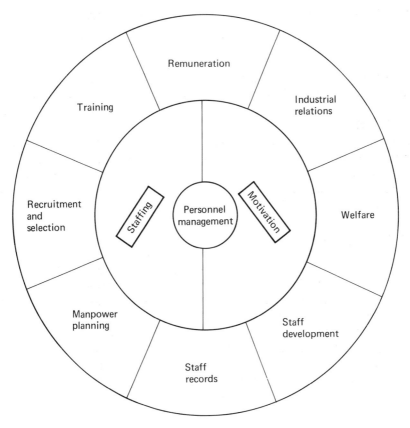

FIG 3

The Predictability of Human Behaviour

Physical scientists are fortunate in that physical laws are highly predictive. Yet human behaviour is also predictable to a certain degree. Thus:

(i) People tend to be motivated to satisfy broadly similar needs.

(ii) People react to frustrating situations in similar ways.

(iii) We can anticipate people's behaviour if we know the roles they are playing at any given time (e.g. sales manager, shop steward, paternalistic employer etc.)

(iv) We can expect people to conform to the social norms prescribed for them by the groups in which they function.

(v) Human attributes including intelligence and physical characteristics fall into a narrow statistical band. For example, the majority of adult males are between 1.60 and 1.80 metres in height, and the majority of adult females shopping in a store would ask for shoes or dresses within a comparitively small range of four or five sizes. It is these limited spans which allow us to mass produce the commodities we desire.

An Introductory Assignment

In order to text your understanding of human relationships before you turn to the case study work you are invited to consider the following problem situations. Tick the boxes which indicate the most appropriate responses. The solutions are given in the Appendix.

1. Tina is Supervisor in a typing pool. One of the girls in the pool, Vicki, is making a habit of coming back late from lunch. The standard of her work is well above average, but Tina is afraid of other girls in the pool acquiring the habit. Which of the following actions would you advise Tina to take?

A. Reprimand Vicki vocally in front of the other girls ☐

B. Send her a brief memorandum reminding her of the authorised times for lunch ☐

C. Have a private word with her, explaining why there is concern ☐

D. Pin a warning on the office notice board for the staff generally ☐

2. A young junior, Patrick, has recently joined the staff. He is quite bright but his job simply requires him to file all the correspondence and produce files as and when required by other members of staff. Some of the staff have begun to complain about his work though they admit he is polite and co-operative. Which of the following would you regard as the least effective action which could be taken by the Office Manager?

A. A strong reprimand ☐
B. An informal chat with him in the privacy of the Manager's office, during which the vital importance of the filing is explained ☐
C. A redesign of Patrick's job so that he does other work as well as filing. ☐
D. Check that he has had the job properly explained to him ☐

3. An Office Manager, John Ackroyd, is concerned at the low morale in his department as evidenced by increased absenteeism and a deterioration in the standard of work. Which of the following steps do you think he should take as a priority?

A. Introduce flexible working hours ☐
B. Give longer coffee breaks ☐
C. Circulate a memorandum warning the staff of the consequences of unexplained absences ☐
D. Consult with his supervisors to find out their views ☐

4. Hilary is a hard-working and efficient member of staff. She has gone into the Manager's office where she is complaining loudly and furiously about the 'incompetence' of Paul, one of the junior executives with whom she has been working. Paul has an excellent record too. The Manager knows that Hilary is having marital problems.
In the circumstances which course of action would you advise?

A. Tell Hilary to come back with some real evidence of the executive's incompetence ☐
B. Listen sympathetically to Hilary but avoid taking sides ☐
C. Positively encourage her to talk over her troubles and offer advice on how she might cope with her marital problems ☐
D. Call in Paul so that the two of them can sort out the problem there and then ☐

CASE 2

Communication in the Workplace

Communication relates to the transmission of thoughts from one person to another. It usually involves the use of language, in which case words are spoken and listened to, or words are written and read by the parties concerned. However, thoughts can also be expressed through facial expressions gestures and visual displays such as diagrams. Oral communication most commonly occurs in face-to-face situations but mechanical media such as radio, telephone or television may be employed.

Within a business organisation the communication process is complicated by the large numbers of people who need to be given instructions or kept informed of developments. The organisation chart below represents a microcosm of the typical large organisation found in industry, commerce and the public service.

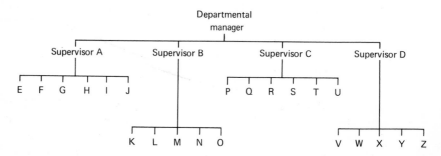

E - Z represent workers, clerks or rank and filers generally

E–Z represent workers, clerks or rank and filers generally. While the chart indicates the organisational hierarchy with its levels of management and its lines of command and responsibility, it also lays out the formal channels of communication. It can be seen that the communication flow within the organisation can be in any one of three directions viz. downward, upward and horizontally (or laterally). Downward communication will normally take the form of imparting commands or giving information — through the various levels of management. Upward communication

16

takes the form of opinions expressed by subordinates, information given by them including recommendations for action, grievances and feedback to the superiors. Lateral exchanges occur between people at the same level in the hierarchy. Thus, departmental managers will consult and confer with each other — formally and informally — and workers will similarly socialise and discuss problems of common moment. The importance of communication to the efficiency of any organisation is widely recognised:

"An organisation cannot function without communication. Communications tie together the component parts of an organisation and impel people to action. In order for group and organisational activity to take place there must be communication among the participants.

Within a work organisation communication serves several functions:

(1) It transmits information and knowledge from person to person so that co-operative action can occur.

(2) It serves to motivate and direct people to do something, as when a supervisor induces subordinates to undertake a project.

(3) It helps to mold attitudes and impart beliefs in order to persuade, convince and influence behaviour.

(4) It helps to orient people to their physical and social environment. Without such orientation, people (employees and managers) would be lost."*

The problems of communicating effectively are also generally admitted by those who have had experience in the business world.

"As production and distribution have become increasingly complex and the size of organisations has increased we have all tended to become specialists. Some of us specialise in production, others in buying, others in selling, and so on. When specialists communicate with others who have a similar background they talk a language all their own. This technical jargon has its advantages, because it saves a great deal of time, yet the more specialised the nature of our work, the more we find ourselves unable to communicate with those who do not possess our specialised knowledge."†

*Dale S. Beach, Personnel — *The Management of People at Work*. Collier MacMillan, London, Second Edition, 1970.
†(R. T. Chappell & W. L. Read, *Business Communications*. Macdonald & Evans, Plymouth, Fourth Edition, 1979).

Not that the problem is simply one of technical jargon. There is a wide variety of possible explanations for communication distortion including a deficiency in the vocabulary of either the receiver or the sender, or both. Certain skills are called for in communicating with people and some are more skilled than others in exercising the required techniques. The perception or emotional state of the receiver is also relevant:

> "No matter how good the communication is within a large organisation, there is sure to be some slippage, so that not every layer knows just what every other layer is thinking. Hence a casual remark at the top is often taken as an order or command at the middle level and soon becomes tradition down at the bottom. For natural reasons the communications down the organisational hierarchy tend to be critical and those up the hierarchy tend to be commendatory. The lower layers tend to filter only the good news back up lest they be held responsible. Accordingly, in large organisations hearing the truth is a major problem for the top leadership."*

If communication within the organisation is a serious problem, external communications are no less critical. In a free and democratic society no organisation can remain insensitive to the reactions of its clients and customers, its suppliers and indeed the public at large. It has to allow for and adapt to the total environment in which it functions, if it is to survive and flourish.

A person making a telephone call may well judge the efficiency of the organisation by the manner in which the receptionist responds. The senior executive will make the important decisions, but the rank and filers will generally make the critical contacts with the public. Both the most senior executive and the office junior have vital roles to play. This is true whether we are talking about manufacturing firms, commercial organisations or public authorities. There is a high level of interaction and interdependence in business. If you think of the business organisation as a human body, Management can be described as the brain, the Sales Department is the mouth (telling outsiders about the products and services offered), the Production Departments are the hands, the Distribution Department is represented as the feet, and Communications are then the central nervous system carrying messages between the various parts of the body. To the extent that the messages are accurate there will be appropriate responses.

---

*B. Berelson and G. A. Steiner, *Human Behaviour.* Harcourt Brace & World, New York, Shorter Edition, 1967.

Information Technology

There have been exciting technological developments in the field of communications. Messages and pictures are beamed from satellites circling the earth and probing distant space. In our homes and workplaces we find ourselves confronted with increasing evidence of the microchip revolution. Smaller and smaller computers appear with sophisticated capacities for the storage, retrieval and processing of information of every sort. In industry, robots on production lines produce motor cars with human intervention almost eliminated. Bankers in London study their viewing screens while their counterparts in New York feed in the latest stock prices and exchange rates through their own visual display units. The visual display unit has become a standard item of equipment in all but the smallest offices.

Word processors store typed communication, figures and text permanently on disk. The information can be retrieved and amended in a matter of minutes. Price lists, advertising material and master copies of letters can be amended quickly and easily. Whole paragraphs and sections as well as individual words and figures can be moved about, revised, added or deleted. The time taken up by preparing and presenting written communication is being considerably reduced. Libraries of information and text are able to be stored and held indefinitely, yet with a capacity for instant retrieval.

As exciting as these developments undoubtedly are they bring their own brands of problem to the workplace. High performance equipment calls for new skills on the part of the operators. The value of old skills becomes discounted. There may also be fewer operators required. Arguably, the new technology contributes to unemployment. Unarguably, the advances in communications science have not solved the fundamental problems we face in our human relationships. Industrial conflict, divorce and war remain to plague us.

The Case Study Technique

The case studies which follow hereafter are an attempt to bridge the gap between theory and practice. They have been designed to give students the opportunity to exercise and develop their communication skills. A wide variety of realistic business problems are posed and the students are invited to solve these problems co-operatively, under the guidance of the tutor.

One should not be misled by the length of a case study. As Geoff Easton points out:

"Cases may be a few sentences or hundreds of pages long.

* From *Learning from Case Studies*, Prentice Hall, London, 1982.

Students taking their first case course usually associate length with difficulty. This is a dangerous principle: many short cases prove to be very taxing. All of the significant detail has been stripped away and the student has to tackle basic issues head on. By contrast, some long cases generate little conflict since there seem to be so few alternatives to choose from. It is never wise to judge a case by its length."

Experience indicates that the layout of the room and the seating arrangements can affect the quality of the discussions. The photograph hereunder shows a group of building society students engaged in case study work at the Dorset Institute of Higher Education. This layout has been found to be efficacious for groups of between 8 and 16 students. Other possible layouts are shown in Fig. 4. Where the conventional classroom layout is unavoidable, the tutor may ask the students to work together in twos (or threes where necessary), reporting their findings back to the larger group. One of the advantages of this treatment is that fairly large groups of students can be dealt with by a single tutor.

PLATE 1

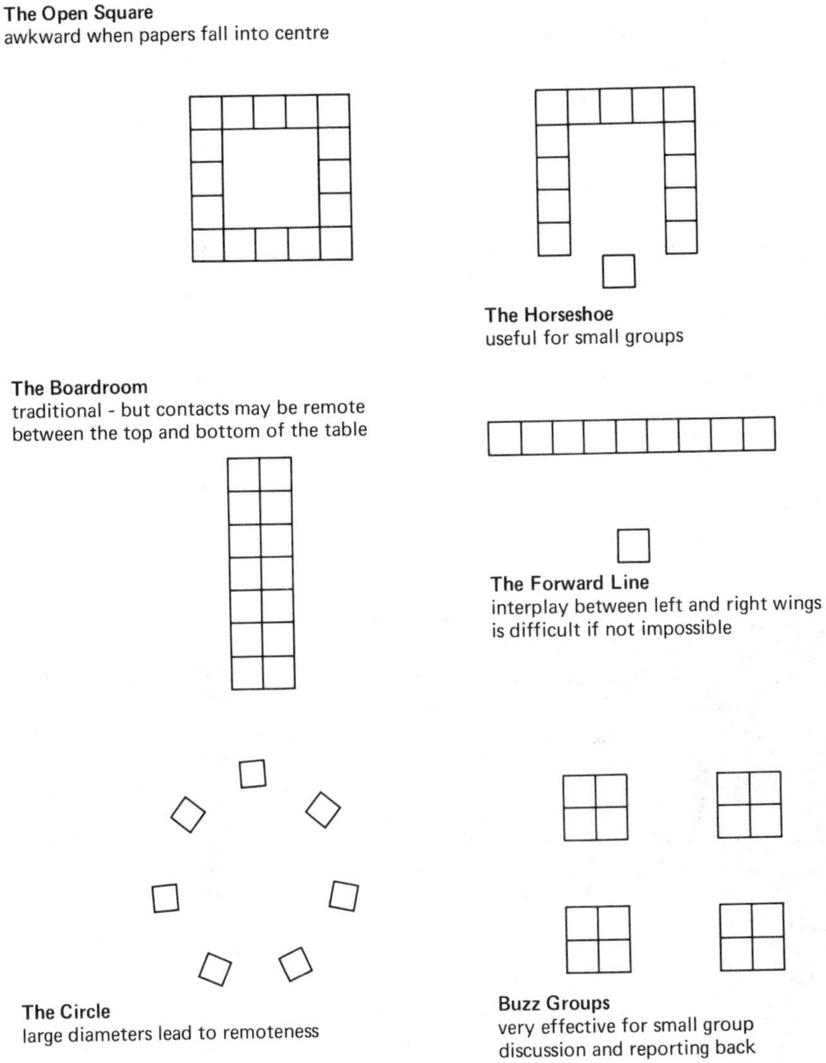

The Open Square
awkward when papers fall into centre

The Horseshoe
useful for small groups

The Boardroom
traditional - but contacts may be remote
between the top and bottom of the table

The Forward Line
interplay between left and right wings
is difficult if not impossible

The Circle
large diameters lead to remoteness

Buzz Groups
very effective for small group
discussion and reporting back

FIG 4

The aims of the programme might be quoted verbatim from the Business Education Council Specification for the Common Core Module 1: People and Communication (August 1977):

"1. Increase the student's effectiveness in work situations, through the development of language and social skills.

2. Contribute to the student's personal development by fostering the ability to communicate with and relate to others, as individuals, in groups and within organisations.
3. Develop the student's skills in dealing with information in various forms, so that he/she is better able to acquire, evaluate and organise it for his own purposes, and to present it in effective form when required, in study and employment.
4. Encourage in the student a sensitivity to the ideas and attitudes of others, an awareness of how these can be affected by the student and other people, and a preparedness to adapt to them where necessary."

The Decision-making Process

An understanding of the principles of decision-making might well be considered as essential to anyone becoming involved in problem-solving case studies. It is not suggested that the varied problems which follow can always be tackled through reference to a rigid formula, but an analytical and objective approach to problems is certainly to be commended.

The principles can be described in this fashion. Whether you are deciding to have coffee rather than tea with your breakfast, to marry Judy rather than Janet, or to buy (or not buy) a particular factory site on behalf of your company, the mechanics of the decision-making process are the same.

Phase I

The full range of alternatives in a given situation need to be considered. What options are available? One of the advantages of group decision-making is that a wider range of options is likely to be envisaged.

Phase II

The advantages and disadvantages of these courses of action must be weighed against each other. For example, Judy is attractive, but Janet's father owns the firm.

Phase III

A choice has to be made between the alternatives. In a business context the choice becomes the most profitable or least costly of the alternatives.

Phase IV

When the best option has been selected the decision has to be implemented.

Organisation
Structure hierachy.

Subordinates are often invited to participate in the first two phases of the decision-making process. They can provide information and discuss a situation usefully with their manager or supervisor. However, the selection of the best option and the implementation of the decision will normally remain the manager's prerogative in view of the fact that he is responsible for any actions taken.

With regard to the case studies here to be analysed the students are invited to go through to the point where the best solution to the problem is decided (Phase III).

The computer is a valuable aid in the making of business decisions. Designed by humans, the computer unsurprisingly simulates the human thinking process but can produce responses far more speedily and accurately. The computer enables us to evaluate a project in financial terms, but some decisions are made on matters such as research and development, staff welfare and training, public relations etc. The costs of these activities can usually be calculated without difficulty, but the benefits are often long-term, indirect, and difficult to assess in purely monetary terms.

There is a danger, therefore, that managements faced with an alternative between, say,

Option A producing easily calculable financial returns *or*
Option B producing indirect and less obvious benefits,

will tend to choose Option A on the basis that "non-monetary" benefit is of lesser, or even nil, value. This is a surprisingly common flaw in decision-making, although in the public sector the technique of Cost-Benefit Analysis is used to account for social costs and benefits which might otherwise be disregarded. The root cause is that we are trained to compartmentalise our knowledge. Industrial relations are unrelated to accounting — even though bad industrial relations can wreak at least as much havoc as an overgenerous distribution of dividends. Similarly, the technical problems of production can be seen as of a different genre to the problems of staff absenteeism — though people may stay away from work to escape from the unrelenting demands of the mass production line.

The following simple case should help to highlight the problem

Alpha Ltd.

Here we have a typical small-to medium-sized manufacturing company. Finances are scarce at the moment (a normal situation in business), and the directors are looking critically at a proposal to spend £200,000 on modernising a canteen. The Personnel Department have completed a survey which indicates that the very poor canteen facilities are a major source of irritation among the majority of the workforce. Personnel Department are convinced that labour turnover would be greately reduced if the modernisation of the canteen took place. Unfortunately for the Personnel Manager his proposals go before the Board at the same time as an alternative project emanating from the Works Manager. If Alpha purchase a new American machine for the Assembly Plant, production can be increased by 10% without increasing the workforce. The machine costs £200,000 and the savings in operating costs are estimated at £50,000 per annum over the next 8 years.

"We don't have any choice, gentlemen," says John Blunt, one of the more forthright directors, "we can't afford to miss this opportunity to cut our operating costs at a time like this. The workers will have to stick to their bangers and chips and like it!"

John Blunt's attitude would no doubt change if the Personnel Manager could show him that the modernisation of the canteen would reduce the costs of labour turnover, absenteeism and lateness to the tune of £60,000 per annum over the next ten years. Such costs may be difficult to gauge accurately, but they erode profits as effectively as the more obvious expenses!

Advantages of Participation

In many cases a manager will have to make a decision quickly and this precludes him from consulting with his subordinates, but when he is able to confer with them the following advantages can be expected:

1. The subordinates will show greater interest in, and identification with, organisational goals. (This should lead to better individual performances.)
2. The quality of decisions will improve because:
   (a) Two heads are better than one.
   (b) One of the problems in choosing between alternatives is the anticipation of reaction by subordinates to the decision, and by bringing them into the decision-making process one is able to learn their reaction *before* the decision is made.
3. There is likely to be a greater willingness to accept authority and a lower resistance to change. People generally have developed an expectation to be consulted about matters which are likely to affect them.
4. There will be fewer grievances, and a reduced tendency to absenteeism, lateness and labour turnover. The experience will be cathartic for the participants.

5. The involvement can be used as a form of training in decision-making for the young executive. It is with this aspect we are primarily concerned here.

The Student's Contribution

The sort of behaviour required from the students, particularly during group discussions can be gleaned from the following extract from the *General and Learning Objectives* laid down by BEC for the People and Communication Core Module:

"On completion of this module the student should be able to:
A. Obtain, select and interpret information
B. Exchange information.
C. Select and use correctly appropriate formats for transfer of information.
D. Identify false argument:
   1. Recognise the place of emotional and non-rational approaches in persuasion and argument.
   2. Discriminate between honest and dishonest use of emotion in argument.
E. Formulate rational arguments:
   1. Give reasons for the opinions he/she holds.
   2. Select and structure his/her arguments.
F. Respond flexibly to personal factors:
   1. Use and respond to imagination and humour in explanation and persuasion.
G. Engage in constructive discussion:
   1. Help others to say what they mean, i.e. identify their difficulties in communicating and offer positive help in overcoming them.
   2. Identify weaknesses in the arguments of others.
   3. Identify points of disagreement."

The case studies which follow are designed to ensure that the student is given appropriate opportunities to achieve these objectives. In group discussions it is particularly important to remember that your colleagues are sensitive human beings. In any business organisation teamwork and co-operation are called for. Acrimony is almost always counter-productive.

Reports

At the end of some of the case studies the students are asked to produce formal written reports. A sample report is given in the Guidelines (Case

No.28). However, there is a merit in students completing less formal reports on the completion of all discussions and the report might take the form indicated on p 27.

The Compendium

At the end of the Guidelines Section there is a Compendium of terms which should be helpful to overseas students and those with little or no practical business experience. There are two optional treatments for the Compendium. Students may either read this before embarking on the case studies or they may choose to refer to the Compendium whenever they are confronted with an unfamiliar term in the case study or in the Guidelines.

Guidelines

A final section is devoted to a fairly detailed set of Guidelines for each of the assignments. These are part of the teaching package but are not intended to be restrictive. They are suggested approaches rather than definitive solutions.

Cameo One

Imagine you are a supervisor employed by a well-known London store and one of your jobs is to deal with complaints received over the telephone. On this particular day you have to deal with the following incoming calls as they are directed to you from the switchboard!

1. "I bought a doll from your Toy Department just over a month ago. My little girl was playing with it to-day and one of the legs came apart. She's only three and she's terribly upset. . . . It cost over £20. . . ." (The caller sounds like the child's mother.)
2. "I came into the store last week to buy a colour television set for my mother's birthday. The young man in your Television Department promised me that he would deliver it this morning and it hasn't arrived. . . . I've tried to get through to him but apparently he's on holiday this week and no-one else knows anything about it. . . . It's a disgusting state of affairs. . . ." (The caller — a male — is obviously very angry.)
3. "My name is Heigerman — Mrs. Heigerman. I have a credit account with the store and I've received a letter this morning from your Accounts Department telling me I'm behind with my payments. . . . But I sent you a cheque over a week ago. . . ."
4. "I came into your store first thing this morning and bought some

Case Study Report/Worksheet

Case No/Title:

Brief description of problem:

Options available:	*Pros*:	*Cons*:

Other points:

Recommendations:

Signed

tights. I gave the girl a £5 note but she gave me change for £1. I didn't realise it until I got out of the store. . . . I went back and the girl was quite rude to me. . . ."

5. "I'm complaining about an advertisement which appeared in the paper last week-end. You said you were having Axminster carpets in your sale . . . from £5.95 a square metre. . . . I came all the way from Orpington and when I got there I found the cheapest Axminsters were £7.95 and you only had three of those. . . ." (It is difficult to tell whether the elderly caller is female or male.)

How would you deal with these calls? What precisely would you say to the callers? Be prepared to accept criticism from the other members of your group.

Who would you inform about the telephone calls within the organisation and what particular follow-ups would you initiate?

Cameo Two

In the same store the Office Manager is being asked to reduce expenditure by 5% during the current year. As a way of making his staff cost-conscious he decides to draw up a schedule showing the different methods of communication and their merits and demerits including cost. He has started the schedule, but now, being caught up in other matters, asks you to complete it for him.

Method	Merits	Demerits
1. Postcard	Easily prepared Cheap	No Confidentiality Sometimes disrespectful
2. Telephone		

CASE 3

Trip to the States

The Drachman Corporation

Tony Phillips has recently been appointed Market Research Manager in the Drachman Corporation. The firm are in the field of electronics producing a wide variety of components for advanced computer systems. Within the past week Tony has been approached in turn by two of his new team, Peter Crisp and Colin Grant. They are both in their late twenties. Both are brimful of ideas and many of them sound good, superficially at least. Peter has been at Drachmans since he left University with an Upper Second in Economics. He has a wife and three children, one of whom is unfortunately retarded. Colin by contrast went to good schools but never got more than a few 'O' levels. It has been suggested that his presence in the Market Research Department is due solely to the fact that his uncle is Sales Director. Nevertheless, Tony finds him personable and persuasive. He makes no bones about being interested in the females, and has admitted to Tony that his marriage is "on the rocks".

John Lampard is in his late forties with a grown-up family. He was on the short list for the job Tony got and is obviously rather resentful still. There is some talk in the office that he is an alcoholic, and he does not seem to be in favour with the Sales Director. However Tony is very dependent on him at the moment because John has a hand in most of the projects which are on the files. Tony is very impressed with his technical knowledge and is trying hard to improve the relationship at the personal level.

Current Problem Requiring Tony's Attention

He has just received the following Memorandum from the Managing Director.

Drachman Corporation

Internal Memorandum

To Tony Phillips,
Market Research Manager.

From Simon Peterson,
Managing Director.

Re: New Aircraft Tracking System

I would like one of your team to make a trip to the United States at the end of next month. The project involves liaising with our parent company in Boston with a view to ascertaining the extent of the market for our new Domino System. I expect the visit to last about a month, but it could be longer — if things go well. Please let me know who you are recommending for the trip by the end of next week. I will give you further details at that time. The project is tagged as a No. 1 priority.

S Peterson

P.S. All expenses will be paid for whichever member of your team is selected.

Tony visits the local pub for a beer and sandwiches and overhears three of the "possibles" for the trip discussing it over their lunch.

Peter Crisp: "I wouldn't mind a free holiday in the States — the wife's got an aunt in Baltimore. A nice holiday for them." (Tony knows that the paid expenses do not extend to a family.)

Colin Grant: "It doesn't fit in with my plans."

John Lampard: "I've got a feeling our new boss has got me down for this one — but just let him try!"

Colin Grant: "Well you're the only one who knows anything about the Domino System."

John Lampard: "That's what I mean!"

Orginisation Chart (Extract)

Managing Director

Sales Director

Sales Manager
U.K.

Market Research
Manager

Sales Manager
Europe

Group discussion

How do you think Tony Phillips should resolve this dilemma? What importance do you think should be attached to office rumours? How could they be verified? What problems *might* develop if normal lines of communication are by-passed (note that the Managing Director is communicating directly with a subordinate's subordinate)?

Assignment

After discussing the problem, each student should complete a Report Form as shown on p. 27

CASE 4

Women at Work

Said I, scorn all burning hot,
In rage and anger high,
"You ignominious idiot!
Those wings were made to fly!"*

The following snippets might help us to understand how recently emerged is the notion of equality between the sexes:

i) In the early nineteenth century a West Country farm worker is reported to have taken his wife to market to sell her.
ii) Until 1888 the Trade Unions in England would not allow women to join their ranks. In that year the London Match girls demonstrated against their low pay and poor working conditions. Their courage won over the support of their male counterparts and they were allowed to join the union.
iii) Mrs. Emmeline Pankhurst was a typical middle-class lady of her day, in many respects, yet in 1910 she was sent to prison for inciting people to "rush the House of Commons". In 1913 she received a sentence of three years penal servitude for blowing up the house of David Lloyd George. What was the "bee in her bonnet"? She was trying to get the same voting rights for women as men had long since enjoyed. She died just before women were given equal voting rights — in 1928.
iv) In 1975 the Sex Discrimination Act was passed making it illegal to discriminate against someone simply because of their sex — in the field of employment.

So that is the end of the story? Or do we still have a long way to go before sexual discrimination is eliminated? How many Presidents of the United States have been female? How many Chief Executives of large business

*From *A Conservative* by the American social reformer Charlotte Gilman (1860–1935).

corporations are women? How many famous inventors, composers, or philosophers have been women? Why the dearth? Some will say the explanation is simple. Men *are* superior to women. Judging by the athletes' performances at the Olympics, men can run faster, jump further, lift heavier weights, and so on. Of course the average male would be left a long way behind by the best female athletes, but if we are to look for a fair assessment, we have to accept the superior muscle-power of the male of the species.

However, male chauvinists may be disturbed to learn that some evidence points in the opposite direction. For example, females have a higher propensity for survival than males. They live longer, on average, according to insurance statistics. In terms of intellect it seems that neither sex has a monopoly. All the evidence points to a broad equality of intelligence, though females tend to mature earlier than males, both physically and mentally.

If women have been dominated by men in the past, the explanation seems obvious. Battles were fought with swords wielded by the more muscular males. When, in industry, workers are still required to use great physical strength, women remain at a disadvantage. You do not have to be a man to drive a car or fly an aeroplane. In many cases, women with their smaller fingers have a greater manual dexterity. The word processor was surely designed for females!

Yet perhaps the contraceptive pill is the final straw which has broken the back of the camel as far as male supremacy is concerned. Women can choose between a career and a family, and many will undoubtedly choose the former. Even those who choose to have children will be able to determine the most propitious moment:

Employment Statistics*

	Men	Women
Total of employees in employment	12m	9m
Average of weekly earnings of manual workers in manufacturing industry at October 1980	£125.58	£76.44

Your First Assignment

Summarise the preceding passage in not more than 100 words. What questions would you need to ask before accepting that the statistics quoted are meaningful?

*Source C.S.O. Monthly Digest of Statistics October 1982

Questions for Discussion by the Group

What sort of jobs do you think men will always be able to do better than
women — and vice versa?

Do you think there is anything else which ought to be done to eliminate
sex discrimination?

How do you see the role of women in society changing in the future?

Case Study
Bestway Supermarkets

Paul Cook is the Manager of a Bestway supermarket on the outskirts of
an East Coast seaside resort. He has recently been promoted to the post of
Area Manager and is looking forward to the challenge. However, he is at
present sitting in his office pondering over the problem of deciding who he
should recommend as his replacement. He has started drafting his
recommendation but he has got no further than the heading:

Bestway Supermarkets
Memorandum

To Mr. K. Gillmore,   From P. Cook, Manager,
    Staff Manager.   Durford Branch.

His dilemma is that he has two very worthwhile candidates for the post.
He likes them both, and he is aware that while one of them will be elated
by a promotion, the other will feel despondent. The one who is rejected
might well look for a job elsewhere, and that would be a pity because they
are both excellent employees with real managerial potential. Paul looks
again at the notes which he has made to help him with his task.

Robin Murray

Age 34. Assistant Manager for past year, previously Assistant Manager
at Tesco (2 years). Wife and three children (aged 2, 6 and 8). Inclined to be
over-friendly with female staff, but is generally popular. Has no academic
qualifications but is studying now at evening classes (BEC Higher National
Certificate). Smart and a stickler for hygiene. Poor with figures — needs a
pocket calculator to work anything out.

Sasha Patel

Age 26. Assistant Manager for past three years. Unmarried — fiancé in the Army — expected to marry when he completes his service at the end of next year. A disciplinarian who has introduced a lot of new ideas, including a customer survey and a new design for Bestway packaging which was accepted by Head Office and earned her a £50 award. Attractive and personable, and a good organiser. Has an A level in Biology (Grade E) and four O levels (in English, Maths, Biology and Religious Studies).

Your Task

Play the role of Paul Cook and, on the evidence available, choose between the two candidates for the job of manager at the Durford branch. Then complete the memorandum to be sent to Head Office with your recommendations. You should also make clear to them how you would propose to cope with the problem of the rejected candidate.

CASE 5

Promotion and Gladys Benson

Northern Lights Insurance Ltd.

Gladys Benson has been with Northern Lights since she left school 20 years ago. Her husband is a senior executive with the Coal Board. They have no children, and Gladys is decidely career-oriented. For the past 18 months she has been acting as Supervisor in the Renewals Department in the prolonged absence of Jack Critchel, the appointed Supervisor. She has not been paid on the Supervisors' Pay Scale, however. She has received instead merit increments which have taken her to within £300 per annum of what she would have received as an appointed Supervisor.

There is a staff of thirty-one, most of whom are female clerks/typists, but there are three males in the age range 20–24. The work done by the Department is simple and routine, merely ensuring that reminders are sent out when premiums become due, but the volume of work is considerable.

David Riggs is the Office Manager, in charge of both Gladys and Jack, and it has now come to his notice that:

(a) Jack is about to be retired prematurely on the grounds of ill-health, in line with company policy. He will receive a full pension as if he had retired at the normal retirement age.

(b) Head Office are advertising for a replacement, in line with company policy, which requires that 50% of all new supervisory and managerial appointments be allocated to external/male candidates.

(c) A number of new Word Processors are to be delivered to the branch shortly. None of the staff have had experience of this equipment which will necessitate drastic changes in the pattern of work and a possible reduction in the numbers of staff required.

Rumours have long been circulating regarding Jack's enforced retirement, and it is obvious that Gladys is expecting to be made up to Supervisor grade. David has found her to be competent and conscientious, if a trifle conservative. She is fairly popular with the staff, especially the few senior women, although some of the younger girls have left recently, complaining about too much discipline.

Gladys has had her widowed mother living with her, and the mother has now been admitted to hospital with a "serious complaint". The news has obviously hit Gladys hard. She has not yet returned to the office.

Group Discussion

1. How do you think David Riggs should deal with this problem?
2. If he wished to recommend a member of his staff, such as Gladys Benson, for the vacant post which of the following factors should he emphasise?
   (a) length of service; (b) age; (c) personality; (d) previous supervisory experience; (e) past work rate; (f) popularity with staff; (g) sexual make-up of workforce.
3. If an external candidate were being considered for the post, to what extent could the Manager depend on a glowing (or adverse) reference given by the candidate's present employer? What information would be forthcoming as the result of an interview with candidates for the post?

Written Assignment

Draft a memorandum to the Personnel Manager at Head Office, Mr. K. Beaumont, informing him of the situation and indicating your recommendations.

CASE 6

Bawls and Smalls

White Cross Laundries Ltd.

When Joanne Laverick joined White Cross Laundries as a Personnel Officer she wondered whether she would be happy with them. In fact she found the job far more interesting than she thought it would be. She was attached to the Executive Director's staff and much to her surprise and delight she was soon given a number of challenging projects.

The organisation is quite large and there are laundries in seven different London suburbs. The smallest has a workforce of 379, while the largest employs over 700. The majority of the workers are female and either unskilled or semi-skilled. All the laundries have one problem in common, that is a shortage of staff — especially female staff. The explanation is probably that the wages are below average for the London area, though the working conditions are generally first-class. Finding staff has become such a serious problem that the Executive Director, Don Beck, has given Joanne a brief to study the possibility of providing crèches at each of the laundries, where mothers can bring and deposit their children while they do their work. The suggestion is that they might be charged a nominal sum for the service. However, the view has also been expressed that the employees who do not have young children should not be expected to subsidise the scheme indirectly.

The composition of the workforce can be gleaned from the following pie-charts which have been provided by the Personnel Department (Fig. 5). A survey has already been completed showing that 34% of the existing workforce who have children under the age of 5 are currently sending a child to a playgroup or are arranging for paid supervision during work hours.

The brief for Joanne reads as follows:

1. Sketch out the benefits that would emerge from a Créche Scheme together with the likely problem areas.
   Indicate the detailed steps that would be necessary to institute such a scheme.

3. Comment on the advisability, or otherwise, of introducing a trial
   créche at one of the laundries in the group as a prelude to a more
   comprehensive scheme.
4. Consider alternatives to the Créche System which might achieve the
   same sort of results.

Analysis of Female Personnel at White Cross Laundries
as at 1 September Last

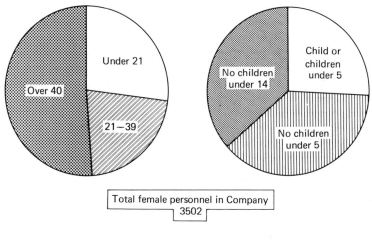

FIG 5

Your Assignment

After discussing the problems posed, write a suitable report to the
Executive Director, giving your recommendations. One of the forms the
report might take is shown on p. 200

CASE 7

Hornet's Nest

K. Sprent Ltd.
John Cowdrey has recently been appointed Office Manager. He has been Assistant Office Manager previously, and having endured a rather autocratic régime himself, he is determined to change the atmosphere now the reins have been passed to him.

One of John's responsibilities is the typing pool. There are eleven girls in this pool. Their ages vary from 16 to 22. They are nearly all audio typists, though two or three are just copy typists. The Supervisor, Alice Bacon, has been with Sprents for just 6 weeks. She was selected from a short-list of five candidates for the job, and John was mainly impressed by her wide experience in similar jobs.

In the past few days there have been complaints from some of the young executives serviced by the pool. They say the service has deteriorated considerably of late. John asks them to be specific and, as a result, he is able to produce evidence of the inferior work for Alice's comments. A number of the letters have more than one word misspelled. In others the corrections have been made but are quite apparent. Another problem appears to be that whereas it used to take 48 hours for a letter to be returned from the pool it is now sometimes taking as long as four days.

Alice obviously feels threatened and begins to harangue the sub-standard staff she has to put up with. She names individual girls who are particularly weak, and recounts incidents which indicate a generally lackadaisical approach to work on the part of many of the girls. At the end of the interview John is glad to see the back of her.

"And she is complaining about *her* staff," he says to himself. However, he has stirred up a hornet's nest. Next day, Alice knocks on John's door. She has brought with her April Anderson, one of the girls from the pool. She leaves the girl outside while she tells John of the complaints she has against her.

"I've warned her before about taking extended lunch hours. She didn't get back till twenty past one, and then she answered me back when I told her off. I've tried to find out how much work she's done all morning and all she has to show me are three short letters. You can see she's even made a mistake on one of these."

"Alright Mrs. Bacon I'll see her."

"I hope you'll back me up Mr. Cowdrey. She's a very bad influence on the other girls."

That was Alice's parting shot.

In comes April Anderson. She is attractive and personable.

"I'm very sorry Mr. Cowdrey," she says. "I did tell Mrs. Bacon the bus back to work was late. She said I shouldn't go home for lunch if I couldn't get back in time. But I've got to have something to eat, and I can't stand the meals you get in the canteen."

"And what about your morning's work?" John asks, brandishing the three short letters.

"I've done more than that," she says, "it's just that I can't trace all my work."

John ponders and pronounces judgement.

"Alright, April," he says, "let's forget all about it this time, but do stay out of trouble in future."

"Thank you, sir," she says smiling sweetly as she leaves, "I don't know what Mrs. Bacon made all the fuss about really."

A few minutes later the Typing Pool Supervisor is asking him what has happened.

John tells her what has been said, with a reasonable degree of accuracy.

"The little bitch!" says Alice, "She never goes home to lunch. I've seen her with a long-haired layabout she calls a boy-friend. They're always together. You're not going to let her get away with that yarn are you?"

How do you think John Cowdrey should have handled this situation? What can he do to improve the future efficiency of the office?

Your Assignment

After discussing the problem together, complete one of the Report Forms, as previously. Compare your Report with that suggested in the Guidelines.

CASE 8

Star Performance

The New Jamaica Hotel

The new Jamaica is one of the smaller hotels owned by the Pearmain Group. Situated in a well-known South Coast resort the hotel has a two-star rating which has been given largely on the strength of the cuisine. The Chef is an Italian, Alberto Ciccetti, who would be able to choose a more highly paid job in almost any of the Group's hotels in Britain or the rest of Europe, but Alberto's daughter has married an Englishman and they are living within a few miles of the New Jamaica, and this accounts for his presence in this particular hotel.

Another distinctive member of the staff is Jane Garner. Jane is the Assistant Manager. She is the first female appointed by the Group to a top Management post. They are watching her carefully to see whether the experiment is a success.

Jane was appointed 10 weeks ago and until now she has been understudying the Manager, but he has just started a fortnight's holiday. During the first week of the holiday Jane is confronted with the following problems:

1. Alberto Ciccetti comes to her office. He is distraught. His daughter has started divorce proceedings against her English husband. He says he has decided to take his daughter and grandchildren (two boys aged 6 and 10) back to Italy at the earliest possible moment.

2. Jane has discovered that the Manager has been charging the hotel more than he has been paying the suppliers, in some instances. In one particular case the invoice presented regularly for poultry and game shows £60, while the cheques paid out each week are for £66. Only two invoices are available (for the most recent payments), but both appear to have been altered from £60 to £66.

3. A young couple on honeymoon have taken possession of Room 29, one of the best rooms in the hotel, with sea views, bath en suite, and balcony. No other room in the hotel has all these features. Another guest has now arrived and claims he booked the room 2 months ago. It becomes obvious that a mistake was made when the receptionist made the booking. Although this guest is shown as having booked

Room 30 the amount of the deposit paid obviously relates to Room 29. The guest is very upset.

4. In the course of a few days two different guests have complained of the loss of personal belongings. One has lost a roll of colour film from a bedside table. The other has lost a nearly-full phial of Chanel No. 5. There has been no suggestion of involving the police by either of the parties, but they are in no doubt that these items have been stolen.

5. Passing through the restaurant at lunch-time — it was crowded — she heard one of the customers complaining about an overcooked steak. The harassed waitress retorted, "Don't blame me. That's the way they cooked it." Her manner was decidedly off-hand, and the customer and his companion were obviously displeased with her manner.

Group Discussion

How do you think Jane should cope with these matters? There are obviously immediate problems to deal with, but do these disclose more deep-rooted deficiences at the New Jamaica?

Your Assignment

Using the resources of your college library find out all you can about the need to post notices disclaiming liability for possessions lost by hotel guests during their stay. When you have completed your investigation, produce a suitable notice for display in a hotel such as the New Jamaica, and explain where such notices should be displayed.

CASE 9

Materialism

"It is easier for a camel to go through the eye of a needle, than for a rich man to enter the kingdom of God."*

We live in a materialist society. Our national goals are clearly defined as economic growth, a healthy balance of payments, and ample gold and currency reserves. If there is a rise in the Index of Industrial Production we are delighted. If there is a run on the pound we are dismayed. As it is at the national level, so it is at the personal level. A man's success is measured by his pay cheque and his bank balance, the value of his house, the age of his car, and the distance he travels for his holidays. His wife can feel pleased or disgruntled according to whether she can boast wall-to-wall carpets, a deep freeze, a dish washer and fashionable clothes.

At both the national and personal levels, it is not absolute terms that concern us. We measure our prosperity in relation to the wealth of others. If they advance at a faster rate than we do, even though we also advance, we are in a state of despair. Thus when Unions are negotiating for pay increases, they are concerned with differentials as well as absolutes.

It is not only a rat race, it is a race for fools — for two reasons. Firstly, there can only be one "richest person in the world". This leaves the rest of the teeming population down the league table — sick and frustrated. Secondly, prosperity in these terms is illusory anyway. Of course we all want material prosperity, but why? Why would I like to own one of the latest, most expensive sports cars? Perhaps I like speed? Perhaps driving it represents a challenge? Perhaps, too, it is pleasurable to draw up at traffic lights beside less admirable vehicles, drawing envious glances from their occupants? And what about the young lady wearing her first real mink coat? Does she get more pleasure out of wearing it in a darkened street, or in the glaring lights of the crowded hotel foyer?

Perhaps we should try to discover the purpose of all this flamboyance in a materialist society. Could it be that what we are really seeking is the approval and respect of those around us? We all have egos. We all need

*From the Gospel according to Matthew 19.24 (The New Testament).

ego food as much as we need our daily bread. And a sure way to satisfy our ego needs is to display the symbols of our excellence — for public approbation. We fail to appreciate, it would seem, that human beings should be evaluated in relation to their personal qualities as well as their personal possessions. What about humility, loyalty, tolerance and sincerity? None of these qualities can be stored in the bank vaults or displayed for public approbation, yet what an impoverished world it would be without them.

There is another drawback to the materialist creed in that the world's resources, at one stage considered to be virtually infinite, are proving to be inadequate for the rapidly-expanded population it has to support. Since this phenomenon has been accompanied by a matching explosion of expectations it seems both as nations and individuals we are doomed to disappointment if we pin our faith on a continually-expanding mass of material possessions.

There is an ugly and vicious circle here, since workers are often forced to walk the treadmill of mass production, performing sub-human tasks in order to gain a higher standard of living — in material terms. Yet they chase rainbows because the material possessions for which they crave are not worth having — in the long run.

The problem is not resolved simply by jettisoning materialism, for we have to decide what to put in its place. If we stop striving for opulence, what *do* we strive for? Do we simply exchange sloth for avarice? Or do we start thinking about the sort of world we would like to live in, and the ways in which we might bring about the changes that are needed?

For Group Discussion

What are your views on this narrative?

Written Work

"Wealth is the parent of luxury and indolence, and poverty of meanness and viciousness, and both of discontent."*

What do you think Plato might have had in mind?

Case Study

Greenacre Dairy

This concern is operating in the Welsh border counties. Bread, milk and eggs are sold through roundsmen working from sixty different distribution

*From *The Republic* by Plato.

points. There are approximately a thousand such roundsmen, and they are paid a basic wage linked to a cost of living index, plus a commission on the following basis:

> 10% on first £300 of sales per week in excess of standard 5% on remainder

(The standard is fixed according to the nature of the round — distance between houses — number of high level flats etc.)

You are a group of executives brought together by the Chief Executive to consider the possibility of supplementing or replacing the existing bonus scheme with one which will offer merchandise rather than money. Sales have been static in terms of physical volume over a long period of time, and the Chief Executive feels that a scheme such as this might generate enthusiasm among the roundsmen.

The scheme envisaged is offered by an outside firm. A glossy catalogue will be provided. Merchandise offered will include such items as:

> Hi-fi music centre (37 points)
> Portable TV set (25 points)
> Two weeks holiday for two in Jugoslavia (42 points)
> Handyman's tool kit (16 points)
> Video cassette recorder (63 points)
> Quartz wrist watch with alarm and calculator (18 points)
> Electric lawnmower (17 points)

The suggestion is that points are awarded for sales above the standard. Points can be exchanged for the prizes at the end of each calendar month. They can be carried over from one month to the next, but all points earned must be spent within a six month period.

According to the firm selling the scheme it pays for itself. Greenacres will be invoiced with the value of the prizes and settle the account annually. The cost of each prize to the firm will be approximately 25% lower than the current market price in the shops. They argue that the roundsmen will be able to choose their own targets and will be encouraged by their families to acquire various items from the catalogue.

"When Dick hears what Harry's got, and Tom's wife hears what Charlie's wife has got, there'll be no holding them" — according to the promoting company.

The Chief Executive, Robert Grierson, asks you to evaluate the scheme and let him know how it might be implemented within the firm. "Let me have a paper on it," he says.

CASE 10

The Welfare State

Department of Health & Social Security
"So long as all the increased wealth which modern progress brings goes but to build up great fortunes, to increase luxury and make sharper the contrast between the House of Have and the House of Want, progress is not real and cannot be permanent."*

Here are three cameos for you to consider. They might help you to decide where you stand on the issue of a Welfare State. To what extent do you think the characters in the situations depicted here should be supported from public funds? Bear in mind that any money paid to them has to be provided esentially from taxes collected from wage-earners.

Cameo 1

Matt has been subject since birth to severe epileptic fits. For a time in his early twenties it seemed as if his doctors had cured him and it was during this "good spell" that he qualified as a telephone engineer and found himself a wife, Rhoda. They did well at first, and bought themselves a pleasant little cottage on the outskirts of town. The purchase money was provided by a building society, of course, and the repayments work out at £200 a month. With both of them at work their income matched their outgoings, but now they have hit trouble. First, Matt started having attacks again. He was forced to give up his job. However, that was not the end of their misfortunes because last week Rhoda's employer — a local dentist — told her he would have to replace her. She was having so many days off that the surgery was not running properly.

Cameo 2

Abe is 28. He has found great difficulty in developing satisfactory relationships with anyone. His mother died when he was two years old and

*From *Progress and Poverty* by the American reformer Henry George 1839–1897.

47

he went to live with a maiden aunt who had little affection for him. He had his first brush with the law at the age of twelve and has since notched up a total of four and a half years in prison for crimes ranging from theft to armed robbery. Surprisingly perhaps, he has not been in trouble with the police for the last eighteen months. A priest who counselled him when he was in prison last time managed to get him a job as a "motel janitor". Abe has worked there ever since, living in one of the smaller self-contained accommodation units. The owner of the motel, who runs a small chain of similar motels, did not bother to tell the staff about Abe's police record, but now they have found out. According to the manager, it is either a case of sacking Abe or losing the rest of the staff. The problem has been exacerbated by the loss of a wallet by a motel guest and some cash which was missing from the till in the reception office.

Cameo 3

Heather is a young married woman who has been plagued by marital difficulties for the past two years. Her marriage is near a break-up and her two children, by a previous husband whom she divorced, would be among those to suffer if this happened. Heather believes that all her problems stem from her slightly deformed nose and she has asked her doctor to recommend that she is given the benefit of cosmetic surgery free under the National Health Service. She could not afford private treatment since her husband is at present unemployed and she only has a part-time job in the local hotel.

Assignment

Discuss these situations and reach a consensus on how you think these problems should be resolved. Then, working as a team, find out as much as possible about succour available to "lame dogs" in our society. Draw up a list of these, distinguishing between those provided by the national government, the local authority, and charitable bodies.

CASE 11

The Good Shepherd

The National Health Service

When Gillian Barlow was appointed a Higher Clerical Officer with the Atherdene District Health Authority she wondered what her new job would entail. There are so many different aspects of hospital administration. Her new boss was John York, the Section Administrator. He called her into his office when she arrived for duty. After the usual pleasantries he got round to the subject of her future role at Atherdene.

"I've had a look at your record since you joined the service," he said thoughtfully. "You've certainly done very well, and according to your references I see you are — and I quote — 'sensitive and sympathetic' among other things." He raised his eyes from the papers and looked squarely at Gillian. "With that in mind," he said, "I'm going to ask you to look after the affairs of the Geriatrics in the district. It's a very responsible job. We've got nearly five hundred elderly and infirm people in the hospitals here — there are over two hundred at Doulton Cross — that's where we keep the worst cases."

Gillian tried not to show her disappointment. Of course it was a vital job, but it was not what she had hoped for. Still, she was obviously the youngest member on the team — as well as the newest — so she could hardly complain.

John introduced her to Judith Grayland, the Administrative Assistant who had been "keeping the job warm" until Gillian arrived. Gillian had a sneaking suspicion that Judith was glad to hand over the responsibility for the care of geriatrics.

"It can be quite interesting," she told Gillian. "Look, here's something for you to start with. These letters came in the post this morning. If you draft the replies I'll check them for you. I'll sign the letter to Mr. Spry. We'll need a power of attorney from him. If he doesn't know what that is you'd better suggest he goes to a solicitor. We've got all the items he mentions. They're with the Securities Section. Of course we can't hand the things over to him just like that." She turned her attention to the second letter. "Oh yes," I've shown this to Mr. York. He says it's been taken up with the District Management Team and they've agreed to use the old television room next to Ward 7 for the salon. You can tell them that — and ask them if they'd like to bring their party along to see the room we've got in mind. Mr. York will sign that letter himself incidentally."

Then Judith got drawn into a conversation with another member of staff allowing Gillian to cope with her task. She looked at the first of the letters.

Rose Cottage,
Glen Drive,
Atherdene.
3rd September 198–

The Hospital Administrator,
Doulton Cross Hospital,
Atherdene.

Dear Sir or Madam,
My Uncle, Thomas Neill, is a patient in the Crosby Ward. He has been there for the past three months and Doctor Hill tells me there is no chance of him ever returning to his home. As I am Mr. Neill's only surviving relative I have spoken to him about looking after his affairs outside the hospital and he has agreed that I should manage things for him. As you will know, he has all his mental faculties but is crippled with arthritis. He owns Rose Cottage and although I am living in it at the present time I shall probably be putting it up for sale, with Mr. Neill's agreement, within the next few months.

However, I am particularly concerned to gain possession of some items which were handed over to the hospital when Mr. Neill was admitted in June. He had three of his late wife's rings which were valued at £350 for insurance purposes, a post office book with a balance of nearly £200 in it, and ten £5 bank notes. I need the money to do some rather urgent repairs. Will you kindly tell me when I can collect these items. Mr. Neill will confirm that you have his permission.

Yours sincerely,

D. Smith

Gillian turned to the second letter. It was brief and she noted that it had been in the office for nearly a week.

35A, Lattimer Court,
Atherdene.
28th August 198–

Dear Mr. York,

I am writing to confirm my telephone call when I told you that my Committee have now authorised me to allocate the sum of £5000 for the setting-up of a hairdressing salon at the Doulton Cross Old Folks Hospital. We hope that this gift will help to make the patients' lives a bit more tolerable.

Some of my Committee members have expressed the desire to visit the hospital in a party and possibly some reporters from the local press will be invited. We cannot get too much publicity for a charity like ours.

The cheque would be handed over in a simple 'ceremony'.

Yours sincerely,

Peter S. Howe

Treasurer, Atherdene League of Friends

Mr. J. York,
Section Administrator,
Atherdene District Health Authority,
Wellington House,
Atherdene.

Your First Assignment

Play the role of the new Higher Clerical Officer at Atherdene and draft suitable letters in response to those confronting Gillian Barlow. When you have completed the drafts exchange them with each other. See if you can find any flaws.

Your Second Assignment

Some jobs in any office are less popular than others. How do you think managers like John York should deal with the problem? Should the younger members of staff be given the more onerous work? Should the manager reward the more hardworking staff with the more interesting posts? Or should there be some sort of rotation? What are the views of the group on this subject? What would be the benefits and drawbacks to the various proposals?

After the discussion, complete a Report Form.

CASE 12

The Lame Dog

The P.X. Corporation

John Fortescue has been with the P.X. Corporation for the past 5 years. During the last 3 years he has been a Senior Systems Analyst. He has worked particularly hard in helping to develop some new high technology software which has found a ready market in the United States and Europe. Recently, he had a rather severe heart attack and has since been in hospital, although he is hoping to go home in a few weeks' time. His wife has visited his office and told his manager it is unlikely he will have the power of concentration to resume his old work. She produces a letter from the specialist which explains how important it is to John's recovery that he does not suffer stress during the period of recuperation. Mrs. Fortescue expresses her gratitude to the firm for continuing to pay her husband's full salary.

"With the house mortgaged up to the hilt and three young children under 8, I couldn't have managed otherwise," she says.

Fortescue's manager is Brian Robinson. Brian reports to his boss who is the General Manager of the Holding Company, Belmore Systems Inc. The General Manager reads the letter and listens to Brian's account of Mrs. Fortescue's visit.

"The trouble is," Brian explains "I got the Board's permission to pay his salary for 3 months, and now I've got to ask for an extension — only for another few weeks presumably."

"You know, Robinson," says the General Manager," I'm very sorry to hear about this fellow — what's his name? Fortescue. I had the same trouble myself a few years ago, but I reckon the corporation's been about as generous as it can be. We've given him 3 months' full pay, but we can't go on and on. And now we know he's not going to be fit even when he does get out of hospital. . . ."

The General Manager is not a man to be trifled with, but Brian ventures to suggest that his subordinate's work was exceptionally good and that a contributory factor to his breakdown, according to the specialists report, was overwork.

The General Manager shakes his head.

"Look Robinson — that's history — we're businessmen — we've got to look ahead. I've said I'm sorry for this fellow, but we're not a philanthropic institution. We're here to make money — not to dole out charity. If you think there's a case for continuing to pay this man's salary — put it in writing — and I'll support it — so long as its based on logic and not emotion."

Group Discussion

What arguments do you think Brian might use to support John Fortescue's case?

Whether you agree with it or not, as a training exercise, put forward a defence for the General Manager's philosophy.

Written Assignment

Play the role of Brian Robinson's personal assistant and draft a brief report for him to be sent to Jeremy Bronson, the General Manager of the Holding Company, and also prepare a letter for his signature to Mrs. Fortescue, explaining the position.

CASE 13

Animal Experiments

Which of the following quotations do you prefer?

"Love all God's creation, the whole and every grain of sand in it. Love every leaf, every ray of God's light. Love the animals, love the plants, love everything. If you love everything, you will perceive the divine mystery in things. Once you perceive it, you will begin to comprehend it better every day. And you will come at last to love the whole world with an all-embracing love."*

or

"Nothing can be more obvious than that all animals were created solely and exclusively for the use of men."†

Your preference will probably reflect your attitude towards vivisection. What is vivisection?

A dictionary definition: "Vivisection — cutting into or experimenting on living animals for scientific study."

Scene 1. A Laboratory in the Midlands

The large white room is filled with identical cages, each of which is clearly numbered. Inside each cage there are up to three white rats. A female laboratory assistant in her late twenties is taking round a new girl who listens intently while their duties are explained to her. They are giving ample helpings of warm bran to the inmates of the cages, most of whom seem in excellent health. As the young ladies get to the end of their round, however, it can be seen that all their charges are not so fortunate. Some show little interest in their food trays. Others are so badly emaciated they can barely be recognised. Their eyes protrude strangely, and if they move at all it is stiffly and painfully.

*From *The Brothers Karamozov* by Fyodor Dostoyevsky (1821–1881).
†From *Headlong Hall* by Thomas Love Peacock (1785–1866)

"Are these ones dead?" asks the new girl pointing to a couple of creatures which are completely motionless.

"No," says her senior, "It will be days before they die."

"What happened to them?"

"They've been injected with a new drug. They'll probably all die in this section. Our job is to monitor their deterioration."

At that moment a Scientific Research Officer comes into the laboratory and looks down thoughtfully at a batch of control cards.

"Fetch me No.898," he says rather brusquely to the assistant.

She opens one of the cages and picks out one of the more obviously sick rats in her gloved hands. She takes it over to the small operating tressle. The scientist is standing there brandishing a scalpel.

"What's he doing?" asks the new girl in a hushed voice as her companion rejoins her.

"A group of them have developed malignant tumours. He has to keep track to see how far the cancer has progressed."

"While it's still alive?"

"Oh yes. It has to be alive."

The new girl raises her eyebrows and watches the proceedings with some misgivings. She is visibly disturbed when the victim emits a weak but pathetic squeal.

"You'll get used to it," says her senior reassuringly, "It's all in a day's work."

"O.K." says the scientist, "You can clear this up whenever you're ready. . . ." When he has written up his notes and left them, the newcomer turns to her experienced colleague and asks simply, "Why?"

"They're testing out a new food additive. If it works they'll be able to keep canned food almost indefinitely. But they're running into some snags at the moment."

Scene 2. The High Court in London

A Barrister (or Counsel), representing the parents of a two-year old girl is making an impassioned plea to the judge. It appears the baby's mother was given a particular brand of tranquilizer by her family doctor during the last six weeks of her pregnancy. As a result, according to Counsel, the baby suffered irreparable brain damage. The parents are claiming £300,000 damages on behalf of their child.

"My Lord," says Counsel, "we have heard the learned witnesses telling the Court that this young child will need someone to wait on her, hand and foot, for the rest of her life. I do not need to describe the agony of her parents. . . ."

Group Discussion

Discuss the issues set out here. What are your views? To what extent can you reconcile your views with those of the other members of the group? To what extent does the problem of animal research impinge on the world of business?

The following is an extract from an article by Adrian Berry in the *Daily Telegraph* of 1st December 1980. He was reporting on some research by two American psychologists, Howard Rachlin of the State University of New York, and Leonard Green of Washington University. They were trying to find out whether rising wages encouraged people to work harder, and in order to solve the problem they studied the behaviour of rats:

"The rats in their laboratory were confronted with two buttons. One, on being pressed, released a quantity of food and the other a quantity of water. The food and the water represent 'wages', and the number of presses needed to obtain them are 'prices'.

The scientists set out to simulate a real economy by manipulating the prices and wages. They cut the amount of food that would appear on each press of the button, and they increased the quantity of water. The result? The animals 'bought' more water and less food, a choice that humans make when commodity prices change.

What happens when prices fall drastically (or when wages rise, which amounts to the same thing) — in other words, if the rats could get very large amounts of food or water for very little effort? They simply lost interest in working, i.e. in pressing buttons.

In the words of the two researchers, 'non-human workers are willing to trade more income for leisure if the price is right.' The experiment, which has also been carried out with pigeons, indicates the existence of a critical level of wages beyond which higher productivity is unattainable."

Case Study

Ling (Pharmaceuticals) Ltd.

This company has made a policy decision to concentrate its research activities on drugs to deal with mental disorders. Philip Kenny, the Research Director who persuaded the Board to allocate a sum of £1,000,000 for fundamental research in this area, argues that as the physical health of the population improves with the help of existing drugs, such as antibiotics, there is going to be an increasing concern over mental health.

One of Kenny's Research Controllers, Mark Lowry, hears about the research allocation and goes to his boss's office where the following conversation takes place.

M.L.: I hope you got my note on my latest project.

P.K.: Yes, I did. Thank you. This "Excenta" drug seems to be a bit of a long shot.

M.L.: I agree. It is. But the initial experiments I've carried out are very interesting. They open up the possibility of controlling behaviour to a degree I never thought possible. "Excenta" isn't a sedative. It's a normaliser. At least that's the way it looks.

P.K.: I'm quite impressed, I admit. You think this might be used on chronically disturbed people?

M.L.: Yes, I do. But I've got to carry out exhaustive tests before I can be sure.

P.K.: I appreciate that. I can't see why you want to set up a laboratory for rhesus monkeys though. £50,000 is a lot of money for equipment.

M.L.: I thought we'd got a £1,000,000 research allocation.

P.K.: Over a 5-year period. And any expenditure has to be vetted by the Special Projects Committee. There are some hard-headed businessmen on that committee.

M.L.: I've got to experiment with "Excenta". I don't see how I can avoid using animals for experiments.

P.K.: I understand that. But there's one man one vote on the committee. You've got to convince the others — not me. All I can suggest is that you put your case personally to the committee. Explain the advantages to be gained by setting up the laboratory. Remember this company has never done anything like this before. And you are not the only one who has got ideas on how to spend this year's allocation. Your arguments had better be convincing. Write out a report and then come along and present it to the committee.

What sort of arguments do you think Mark Lowry might use?

Assignment

One of your number should be chosen to play the role of Mark Lowry. The other members of the group then play the role of the Special Projects Committee and listen to his plea for the research allocation.

SECTION II

Problems Centred on Communication

CASE 14

The Distortion Barriers

An Exercise in Communication

Follow these instructions carefully:

1. The tutor will give a selected member of the group a copy of a short newspaper article. The article will be read and absorbed by the selected person for a maximum of two minutes. It will then be returned to the tutor. The selected person will then go out of the room in company with a second member of the group. Outside and so as not to be heard by the others, the first person will explain the contents of the article to the second person. The second person will listen but not ask questions.
2. The first person will now return to the group and a third person will join the second person outside the room. The second person will tell the third person the contents of the news item as it was told to him/her. Again, the third person will listen but not ask questions.
3. The second person will now rejoin the main group and a fourth person will join the third person outside. The process will be repeated as before.
4. Meanwhile, the tutor will now give copies of the article to the remainder of the group for study.
5. The third and fourth persons now return to the room. The third person rejoins the main group. The fourth person sits facing them and explains to them the contents of the article. The remainder of the group then ask questions designed to discover just how much of the original message has been received and understood by the last link in the communications chain.

What did you learn about communication from this experiment? How do you think the message could have been transmitted more effectively? Bearing in mind that there are often four levels of management in a business organisation, what do you think are the implications?

CASE 15

A Free Press

"None can love freedom heartily, but good men; the rest love
not freedom but licence."*

What is meant by the term "a free press"? One interpretation would be "a
situation wherein people might write and publish what they like, when they
like, and how they like. . .". This is a rather *unrealistic* definition,
however, because such freedom is only possible in a state of *anarchy*. What
we need to add to the definition, perhaps, is the phrase ". . . within the
parameters of the law". Even with that *refinement*, difficulties are encountered because all national presses can be said to be "free" in these terms —
though they are functioning in the most restrictive and illiberal of societies.

A more perceptive definition might then be "a free press exists when it is
not essentially controlled by the state or by an unacceptably limited number of individuals, and when views can be expressed which are openly
critical of the government — and other institutions". The rights of free
expression should include the right to criticise, so long as the criticism can
be supported as "fair comment on a matter of public concern". If anyone
considers their reputation has been damaged by something which has been
published, they can bring an action for libel in the courts, and claim
compensation (or damages) against the *perpetrators*. The term "libel" is
reserved for written *defamation*. Where the defamation is oral the term
"slander" is used. The opposite of a free press might be described as a
state-controlled press, and in this case, all news items are either
promulgated for, or vetted by, the existing government. It could be said, in
this case, that newspapers and magazines are allowed to *disgorge* only such
information as the government wishes to be known by the public. Of
course, even where freedom to criticise exists it may be that the channels of
criticism are controlled by too few individuals. This is one reason why some
who value democracy are dismayed when a good newspaper is forced to
stop publishing as a result of falling circulation (sales). Or when one
newspaper is taken over by another publishing group. While the "Press" is

*From *Tenure of Kings and Magistrates* by John Milton (1608–1674).

intended to include newspapers, magazines and books, it may be noted that an essential difference between these media is the time element. Since newspapers print news and views at comparatively short notice, they may be regarded as the *mainstay* of a free press.

The principal advantage of a free press is that it curbs the *omnipotence* of a government. Without this institution the government remains the sole *arbiter* of what information the public is to be given, and what information is to be withheld. In a democracy, by definition, power is diffused. A free press is one of the means by which this *diffusion* is fostered.

The principal drawback to a free press is that since it is organised on a commercial basis, it depends on the making of profits. Thus, editors will have to concern themselves with circulation figures. They may be forced to *pander* to mass tastes and the lowest common denominators. Worse, if the press is obliged to trade in sensationalism, the public may be given a false and deformed image of itself. If normal decent behaviour is inadequately *lauded*, while corruption and *unethical* behaviour monopolise the communications media, the public may come to accept the deformities and abnormalities as normal standards of behaviour — and adjust their actions accordingly. This could be instrumental in lowering the moral standards of society.

Your First Assignment

Explain the meaning of the words in italics. Use your dictionary to check your answers. Then express these ideas in your own words.

Case Study

The Daily Clarion

Jeremy Wright is the Editor of the Daily Clarion, a daily evening newspaper which circulates in the Midlands. He has just finished his evening meal and has retired to his study. He opens his brief case to study some of the problems he has brought home with him.

1. A letter has been received from the Managing Director of an engineering company sited on the outskirts of Birmingham. He complains about a recent article in the paper which was highly critical of one of the company's products, a specially designed ramp for cars. The implication was that the product could cause death or serious injury in certain circumstances. The Managing Director reminded the Editor that the engineering company had spent well over £1000 on advertising in the Daily Clarion during the past six months. All future advertising would be cancelled unless the Editor printed a retraction.

2. A notorious criminal has just been sentenced to life imprisonment. He was finally caught after killing a customer in a local bank he was robbing. One newspaper is known to have paid a very large sum of money to the estranged wife of the murderer for an exclusive story of her life with him. A letter has now been received by the Clarion from someone representing the 19 year-old stepdaughter of the murderer who claims to have even more macabre details to disclose. The letter ends "The fee for this exclusive story would be open to negotiation."

3. A letter has been received from a Mr. P. Ogden, who is complaining about a new town by-pass road scheme which would necessitate the demolition of his cottage. He would be paid compensation but says at 80 years of age he does not want to move out of the cottage which has been his home for the last forty five years. Mr. Ogden's complaint against the Clarion is that, though he has written thirteen letters to them pointing out the deficiencies of the proposed by-pass, not one of his letters has been published. But numerous letters have appeared in the Open Forum section of the newspaper supporting the proposals. The Open Forum section is in the hands of a sub-editor and Jeremy Wright has always given him a free rein in deciding which correspondence to include.

For Group Discussion

How do you think Jeremy Wright should deal with these letters?

To what extent do you think a free press is vital today? Do you think newspapers perform a public service? Are there any exceptions? Do you think *any* restrictions should be placed on the printing of newspapers, magazines or books? How would you impose restrictions?

Has television eliminated the need for newspapers? Do they both serve the same market — or are there distinctions?

What do you think would happen to a society such as ours if the government of the day took over control of the press?

Written Assignment

Play the role of Jeremy Wright and make some notes which will be useful when he deals with the problem letters back in his office.

CASE 16

Fresh Pastures

Blue Circle Industries
A news item from the Daily Telegraph of the 29th August 1981:

"A company is to assist employees it has made redundant to start up their own businesses. Others who have left for other reasons may also benefit. Blue Circle Industries, the cement group, is to launch a trust to help assess the merit of each business, assist in obtaining finance, and give advice as the business develops.

The trust will also consider helping non-employees where their businesses would employ redundant Blue Circle workers. It is to be based at Blue Circle House, Gravesend, and the chairman of the trustees will be company director Mr. Tony Jackson."

Kevin Longmore is 42 and has recently been given a redundancy notice by his employers. As always when there is a crisis in the family, he calls a Council of War. His wife, Jacqueline, is a nurse. His son Adam, aged 19, is training to be an accountant. His daughter Elizabeth, aged 17, is on a secretarial course at the local technical college. They join forces around the dining room table and the following dialogue takes place:

Kevin: Well, you know why I've called you together this evening. I've lost my job. Mind you, it could be a lot worse. I've had a chat with the Union rep. and the Personnel Manager, and I calculate that my redundancy pay and compensation from the firm will come to about £7500.

Liz: That's a lot of money.

Jacqui: It's got to last a long time too.

Kevin: That's true. Anyway, I showed Mum the piece in the newspaper, and Blue Circle will help me to set up in my own business as long as I can put up a good case. I don't intend to stay out of work for the rest of my life, so I've got to do something.

Adam: What were you thinking of doing, Dad? I know you can turn your hand to anything practical.

Kevin: I haven't come up with any ideas yet. That's why I've called this little meeting. If two heads are better than one — four heads should be better still.

Adam: Are you limited to the redundancy pay for your capital?

Kevin: Not if I can get the support from the Blue Circle Trustees.

Jacqui: We could sell the house.

Liz: Where would we live?

Kevin: I'm not planning to sell the house unless we have to, but it would fetch about £30,000 I suppose, less the £15,000 mortgage we've still got to pay off.

Adam: Look, Dad, we need time to think about this.

Kevin: I agree. All I want you to do is to put your thinking caps on.

Your Assignment

Assume that the Longmore family are living in your neighbourhood. What ideas might they come up with? Spend the coming week thinking over the problem — in much the same way the Longmores would have done. When you have exchanged ideas at the end of the week, choose the best suggestion and then prepare a letter to the Chairman of the Trustees seeking his support for your scheme. Only a brief outline of your proposal will be required initially.

CASE 17

The Ice Age Cometh

Tolfree Central Heating

After a long spell in the Royal Engineers, Paul Tolfree used his gratuity together with a sizeable bank loan to start up a gas central heating business in his native Poole. The business was slow to develop but Paul has now designed a new mini-boiler unit which has dramatically reduced the cost of installation. As a result, the business is starting to expand and he has trebled his workforce over the past few months. Another reason for his success is that he offers an economic double glazing service in combination with the central heating.

Paul has decided to advertise on a larger scale than hitherto and has contacted a local advertising agency with this in mind. The following letter arrived in his post one morning.

The Dolphin Advertising Agency,
Dolphin House,
Poole, Dorset.

10th September 198–.

Dear Mr. Tolfree,

I have worked out a few ideas for the advertisements in the local press and enclose some samples. They are rough sketches at this stage to minimise costs, but if you like any of them the art work can be elaborated.

I would suggest taking a weekly spot in both the Evening Echo and the Western Gazette for a continuous period of sixteen weeks. My feeling is that we should use the same material for the whole of this period, but much depends on how strongly you favour any of the designs. The other dimension to the campaign at this stage will be a regular morning slot on local radio (2CR). I suggest a 25 second slot — repeated within the hour. If you have any thoughts of your own,

---

67

let me know. Clients often like to devise their own material, though a professional tape will have to be prepared eventually.

In any case I would welcome your thoughts on the art work as soon as possible, so that our artist can make any refinements required.

Yours sincerely,

K. Rebbeck

Katrina Rebbeck

Your Assignment

Without referring to the other members of your group, in this instance, play the role of Paul Tolfree and draft a suitable reply.

An Optional Assignment

If you have the facilities available prepare a tape for the advertising slot on 2CR. Compare your efforts and decide which of them would be most effective.

THE ICE AGE COMETH **J**
HOW ARE YOU PREPARING FOR IT?

K HOW DO YOU INTEND TO KEEP WARM
NEXT WINTER?

It's no joke when you are trying to keep warm within a budget. If you want serious advice from the central heating experts complete the coupon below and we will send you our free booklet "Central Heating - The Tolfree Way". It could give you a snug winter!

Tolfree Central Heating Ltd.,
Baiter's Creek, Poole.

Please send me without obligation your booklet "Central Heating - The Tolfree Way".

NAME. . . . .

ADDRESS. . . . .

. . . .

Relax and let the experts do the hard work for you. Tolfree Central Heating Ltd. have the technology you are entitled to expect coupled with a price you can afford. Send for our free booklet and decide for yourself how to cope with winter.

Tolfree Central Heating Ltd.,
Baiter's Creek, Poole.

Please send me without obligation your booklet "Central Heating - The Tolfree Way".

NAME. . . . .

ADDRESS. . . . .

. . . .

There's no better way of showing the 'little woman' how much you care for her than by giving her something to keep her warm and snug. Buy her a mink and you will have to take her out so that she can show it off to her friends. Install one of our Central Heating Systems and you will not only be saving on your heating bills. She will never want to leave the cosy love-nest. Seriously though you must send for our free booklet - look through it together - and decide how you want to spend next winter.

To Tolfree Central Heating Ltd., Baiter's Creek, Poole.

Please send me without obligation your booklet "Central Heating - The Tolfree Way".

NAME. . . . .

ADDRESS. . . . .

H IF YOU WANT TO KEEP

THE WIFE HAPPY

YOU COULD BUY

HER A MINK

BUT THERE ARE OTHER WAYS
TO KEEP HER WARM!

FIG 6

CASE 18

A Shadow of the Truth

Sunshine Tours Ltd.

Cameo One

You have never heard of Bonavita, but the advertisement makes it sound marvellous, and the price is competitive. You turn up at the Travel Agents and are met by a bright and helpful young man.

"A fortnight in Bonavita," he says, "I don't think we've got any vacancies. The seats were booked almost before the advert went in. Yes, this one is very popular. It was the same last season."

Just then the telephone rings and he asks to be excused.

"Hold on," he says, putting his hand over the mouthpiece and turning back to you. "We're lucky. There's a cancellation here. A double booking. Two weeks did you say? From the 14th?"

How would you react as the story unfolded?

An Alternative Ending

You have decided to spend your holiday in Bonavita. It sounds a marvellous place. The bright young Travel Agent appears. "Bonavita," he says, "we don't get many enquiries for Bonavita. In fact," he takes out a very dusty file marked with the name of the resort. "You are the first one to ask about it in the two years we've had it on our books."

How would you feel about that?

Cameo Two

You are visiting a street market — the sort which was common in the 1920s and 1930s. One of the traders is making a lot of noise and collecting quite a crowd round him. He is selling tea sets.

"Take a look at the quality," he says, "go on pick 'em up and look at 'em. Pass it round Charlie. I'll tell you what I'll charge you — not eight pounds — not seven pounds — not even six pounds — I must be mad — five pounds."

A few of the crowd seem on the verge of buying, but they sense there may be something else to their advantage yet. The trader looks at his audience in disbelief.

"I've got to clear them out," he says, "I've got nowhere to store them." He looks at the crowd hopefully and when they show no sign of helping him out by buying them, he turns to Charlie.

"Fetch out those Swiss jewelled watches," he says.

Charlie gives out a few "buts" to indicate his doubts about the way things are going.

"Have a look at this watch," he says cataloguing its features. "Pass it round, Charlie."

The audience look it over suspiciously, but it looks a good enough timepiece. What is he going to say next?

"Alright," he says, "I *am* mad. Take the watch and the teaset — I've only got six of the watches remember — so don't complain because your money is stuck in your purse lady — the teaset and the watch — ten pounds for the two to the first six customers!"

The crowd push forward with their notes waving in the air.

If you were among them would you be tempted? The question is not whether you would buy, but would you feel the pressure of temptation? A bit like the Gold Rush?

The Application

Sunshine Tours have entered into a contract with an operator who is offering Moroccan Atlantic Coast Holidays with individual chalets, communal dining halls and clubs. It will be the first time that the South Agadir Holiday Village has been occupied by guests. The buildings have only just been completed, and staff are still being recruited.

You represent a team of executives from Sunshine Tours who are now asked to make specific recommendations with regard to the promotion of the South Agadir Holiday village.

One of the directors has visited the site and his notes are available.

Notes on South Agadir Holiday Village

Should be completed by the start of the season. Plenty of local labour available. Main attractions — excellent climate throughout the year — and scenically beautiful — backed by the Atlas Mountains. Main detractions — isolated — and there was an earthquake here some years ago though no sign of it now. Railway is unreliable and uncomfortable. The camel trains are better!

Camp is 3 km from town, virtually in the desert. Chalets of two types. About 100 will have two berths and 200 will have four berths.

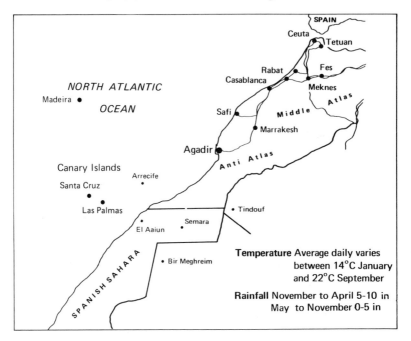

The map shows the following labels:

SPAIN
Ceuta
Tetuan
Rabat
Fes
Casablanca
NORTH ATLANTIC
Meknes
Madeira •
OCEAN
Atlas
Safi
Middle
Marrakesh
Agadir
Canary Islands
Anti Atlas
Arrecife •
Santa Cruz •
•
Las Palmas
• Tindouf
Semara
•
El Aaiun
SPANISH SAHARA
• Bir Meghreim

Temperature Average daily varies
between 14°C January
and 22°C September

Rainfall November to April 5-10 in
May to November 0-5 in

FIG 7

Optional extras Sea voyage to Canaries? Week-end in Marrakesh?

Your Assignment

After discussing which type of people are likely to be attracted to this camp, complete a Case Study Report evaluating the options. Then design an advertisement which is to appear in the back pages of a well-known Mail Order House catalogue. One half of the page will be given over to photographs of the site and the surrounding landscape. You should concentrate on the accompanying narrative which is aimed at persuading the reader to embark on this holiday. Your approach will no doubt vary according to which groups you think will be interested. The size of the printed words can vary. Limit yourself to 100 words in all. You can ignore the terms and application forms which will be disclosed elsewhere.

Bearing in mind the groups you are primarily catering for, which other magazines and papers would be useful advertising media?

CASE 19

"As Madame wishes . . ."

Gustav's Fashion House

This concern has been selling clothing to a small, select and wealthy clientele over a long period of time. It has always closed at 6.00 p.m. but the new manager believes it would be profitable to stay open until 9.00 p.m. on two nights a week — Tuesday and Friday. Under the present system, each of the sales staff have their own clientele and are paid on a commission basis. The staff is as follows:

Manager, 2 Senior Salesladies, 11 Salesladies
1 Workroom Supervisor, 3 Needleworkers

The store is part of the International Fashion Houses Group and the Manager has sought the advice of his Head Office.

You represent a group of Trainee Managers who have been bought together by the Personnel director to consider the problem likely to be encountered and to produce a practical solution.

The Manager's Report to Head Office reads:

"An analysis of our sales shows a steady decline over 5 years. I believe this to be caused by the rising age of our established clientele, and the reluctance of their daughters to join them when they visit the store.

"We are also having difficulty in finding workroom staff of a satisfactory calibre.

"Added to which, we have lost at least one valuable client during the last week because she was fined for parking on double yellow lines. These have now been introduced immediately outside our salon.

"I have not discussed these proposals with any member of my staff in case they offend group policy, but if they meet with your approval in principle, I should welcome your advice on how to implement the changes. My staff are difficult enough — without any need to provoke them."

Signed David Frenchman

Group Task

Discuss the problem and attempt to find an acceptable solution.

Written Work

When you have completed the discussion, choose appropriate forms of communication by means of which (a) clientele, and (b) staff, might be acquainted with the problem and the ideas being floated, bearing in mind their ideas and reactions need to be known before any changes are made.

A Second Group Task

Look at the written work which has been produced and decide which approach is likely to be most effective. Any weaknesses can be identified, but all criticism should be constructive.

CASE 20

Hygiene on the Agenda

Soft Drinks Ltd.

This is a small concern with capitalisation under £100,000 and a workforce of about 350 engaged on producing a single-brand fruit drink, almost exclusively for local seaside markets. You represent a group of Directors attending a regular monthly Board meeting, and the Agenda includes the following matters requiring your attention:

1. The General Manager, who is unavoidably absent from this meeting, reports three cases of customers complaining about dirty bottles. In two of the cases he was able to placate the parties, but in the third case the Health Inspector has become involved.
2. The General Manager has produced a formula for a new drink with slight alcoholic content aimed at the younger element frequenting pubs. It has to be decided what the next step shall be.
3. One of the company's best customers (a local authority Beach Service) has cancelled its contract, without explanation.
4. Out of a total of seventeen inspectors on the production line five of the all-male force have left within the last month; three gave as their reason "fed up with the job".

Additional Information

Each bottle is visually inspected as it passes the Inspectors on a conveyor belt. There have been attempts to develop mechanical inspection devices, but these have either proved ineffective or too expensive. The Inspectors are comparatively highly paid.

Group Task

Play the role of the Board of Directors of this company and deal with the items on the Agenda. Formal resolutions will have to be proposed and passed by a simple majority of Directors present. In this way the Board makes its decisions. One of your number will need to be elected Chairman to control the proceedings. Another will need to act as Secretary, keeping a record of the proceedings in the form of minutes.

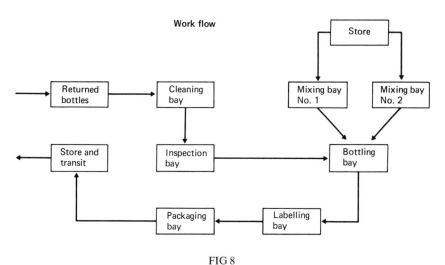

FIG 8

Individual Task

Without referring to the other members of the group, draft a letter in reply to one of the customers who has complained about a dirty bottle. She is Mrs. J. Arkwright, of 32, Station Approach, Ludlow, Salop. In her letter she says, "When my small son emptied the bottle I saw to my horror some thick grease (?) left at the bottom. I have kept the bottle if you want to see it, but I am just horrified to think what that substance might be."

Using the resources of your college library find out what the legal position is in this situation.

CASE 21

Limited Liability

Oliver & Reece

Juliet Stevens is a private secretary working for Peter Oliver, the senior partner in a firm of chartered accountants. One morning he is dictating some letters to her when he receives a telephone call from one of his most important clients.

"I'm sorry Julie," he says, "I have to go out to Mr. Maxted now I'm afraid. But never mind. There's only one more item to deal with. Perhaps you could draft a letter for me to sign when I get back."

He passes over the letter which needs her attention. It reads:

The Barnaby Boutique,
31, Quigley Street,
Dunford.
8th September 198—.

Mr. P. Oliver,
36, Bank Chambers,
Dunford.

Dear Mr. Oliver,

Thank you for the accounts which I received a few days ago. I was very pleased with the results for my first year in business. It was a bit nerve-racking initially but I have got used to accumulating bills now. I have a feeling the next year is not going to be quite so easy. I am beginning to get quite a stock of dresses on my hands and reckon it will soon be time for an "autumn sale".

I mentioned when I came to see you that I was buying a flat with some of the money that my father left me in his will. I was in with my solicitor the other day and while we were discussing the property I mentioned about the boutique. He said something about forming a limited company. I had so much on my mind and anyway lawyers

---

77

make it all sound so complicated I thought I would ask you for advice. Do you think I ought to form a company? I would be grateful for any advice you can give me. Meanwhile,

Best wishes,
Yours sincerely,

Pam Quigley

Your Task

Prepare a suitable letter for signature by the Senior Partner. Then exchange the draft with another member of your group. Comment on each other's work critically and constructively.

CASE 22

Fair Shares for All

Mancini Warehouses Ltd.
This company has three sizeable Cash and Carry Warehouses in operation. In each case the Warehouse is close to a northern industrial town. The principal lines traded are grocery and provisions, but new lines are constantly being introduced. John Mancini, the Chairman and principal shareholder, has bought a fourth Warehouse, this time on the outskirts of an East Midlands town — a group of disused aircraft hangars which are being converted with the aid of a long-term bank loan.

The key staff have been drawn largely from the existing business, but the operations to date have been on a much smaller scale than is now contemplated. However, a Chief Executive has been appointed to develop and control the Mail Order business and he has plenty of experience in the type of retail operations now contemplated. Adrian Frisby has been with two different Mail Order Houses, and was Chief Buyer (Clothing and Footwear) in his previous appointment. The new business is being organised in six Divisions. The break-down is indicated below:

Chief Executive
(Adrian Frisby)

Clothing & Footwear	Electric & Hardware	Textiles & Furniture	Miscellaneous & New Lines	Personnel	Finance & Accounts

There is to be a national advertising campaign in the press and on television. Attractive glossy magazines are to be produced which will be circulated to anyone asking for them. There will be no agents, but a 10% discount will be offered on any orders exceeding £30. Prices are aimed at being so competitive that the volume of business will not be reduced although credit terms are only available on orders over £100.

Adrian Frisby's nominees have been appointed as Chief Buyers in the Clothing and Footwear, and Textiles and Furniture Divisions, while John Mancini's son, Vincent, has been put in charge of the Miscellaneous and New Lines Division. This latter Division will aim to seek out new markets.

79

In fact, it is already mooted that a substantial section of the Catalogue should be devoted to Package Holidays and plans in this direction are well advanced. It is on the question of the Catalogue that the first serious frictions in the new team have arisen. A dispute has occurred as to what proportion of the Catalogue each of the selling Divisions should have. A debate has also developed concerning the order of precedence in the Catalogue for the different categories of goods. The two Chief Buyers who were previously employed by Mancini have brought the confrontation to his notice, and he has suggested the setting up of a formal Catalogue Committee with himself as Chairman, Adrian as Vice-Chairman, and all Divisional Heads other than Personnel as members. One other member is proposed, viz. Max Anning who is being brought into the organisation as Chief Photographer. The purpose of the Committee will be to allocate space in the Catalogue.

Your Assignment

Referring bask to Cases 1 and 2 and working in twos or threes, draw up a list of the advantages and disadvantages of using a Committee in a situation like this. Do you see any special problems here?

When you have completed the task, compare your lists with those shown in the Guidelines.

CASE 23

Fleet Street — Next Stop

Montford Bakeries

Mark Telford, the Personnel Manager, is trying to persuade his Managing Director to budget for an initial sum of £5000 to be spent on producing a monthy staff magazine claiming that it will improve communication generally in the firm. The Managing Director is interested enough to ask for further details. He has sent a memorandum to his Personnel Manager which asks specifically:

1. What can be expected from the investment?
2. What would the contents of the magazine be — in broad outline?
3. Who would be responsible for compiling the magazine?

Telford now comes to you and asks you to deal with these queries. "Just let me have your ideas," he says, "there's no need for a formal report. I'll do that. You give me a brief note of the way you think we should tackle it. Why not start off by collecting some samples of staff magazines and news-sheets from other organisations. Study them critically. Perhaps they'll give you some more ideas."

Background Information

Montford Bakeries employ 2375 staff in total. The majority of these work in the factory producing bread, cakes and dog biscuits. The staff includes a sales force of some 67 travelling representatives and 350 or so roundsmen using delivery vans.

There are 90 people employed in the offices which are on a site across the road from the factory.

Eighty-five percent of the workers in the factory are women — the majority under the age of 25.

There is a considerable amount of shift-work, the bulk of the late shifts being done by men and older women. Personnel Department's records show that there are over 100 married couples in the workforce.

Average period of employment: women: 6 months

men: 5 years

CASE 24

Staff Opinion Poll (Part One)

Blue Shield Insurance Ltd.

Scene One

The office of Tom Selwyn who is Personnel Manager of Blue Shield. Tom is talking to recently appointed Martyn Fraser, a Personnel Officer engaged on Research projects. The subject is Employee Attitude Surveys and Martyn is trying to persuade his boss that such surveys have a value.

Tom: I still think you can get more from wide-awake line managers than you can from a survey. People just put down answers without out really caring.

Martyn: Let me put it this way. If the Conservatives lose ground in the Public Opinion Polls do you think they can close their eyes completely — say it doesn't mean anything? It *may* not mean anything, but they're fools if they don't take note of apparent changes in their support. Or again, would you advocate the introduction of a new type of insurance contract without testing the market in one way or another? Indeed, shouldn't we be testing the market all the time. Isn't that what market research is all about? The market is changing all the time and if we don't adapt ourselves to these changes we are in trouble — in the long run. I'm only suggesting we do some market research on our staff — using the same technique, basically, as the market research boys use.

Tom: So what do you want to do?

Martyn: I suggest we produce a pilot survey, in the first place. Ten questions. You know the sort of thing — "What do you think of your manager or supervisor?" — they have to tick one of five boxes indicating their viewpoint — "Very good" — "Above average" — It's not difficult to think up questions. The problem is getting five equally-spaced responses.

Tom: Alright. You produce a questionnaire and I'll have a look at it. I'm not promising anything mark you. But if it looks reasonable when you've prepared it we'll see what the next stage is.

82

(*Exit Martyn Fraser with a rather determined look on his face*)

Your Assignment

Martyn to turns to you, his colleagues for support. Help him to draw up a list of questions and responses suitable for presentation to the Personnel Manager.

CASE 25

Staff Opinion Poll (Part Two)

Blue Shield Insurance Ltd.

Scene Two

The office of Tom Selwyn again. Martyn Fraser has brought in his proposed Employee Attitude Survey, which Tom is presently studying.

Tom: Yes. That looks interesting, Martyn. You haven't said whether the respondents are going to put their names somewhere on the questionnaire. Nor how it's going to be distributed and collected. How many staff are we going to canvas? Is it going to be a random sample — or stratified? We've got to be quite clear in our minds. We're going to sell this idea to our General Manager — and he's got both his feet firmly on the ground — I promise you. What use is the Survey? What can we get out of it?

Martyn: You want a sort of cost-benefit analysis from me.

Tom: That's the sort of thing. I presume your approach will be that if you can find out what's wrong with working for Blue Shield you can then try and do something about it. Incidentally, I know of one firm that's trying to develop an Index of Morale based on Surveys like this.

Martyn: How does that work?

Tom: The responses are scored and totalled. The total serves as a base index. Do you get the idea?

Martyn: Scored? You mean 5 for very good — 4 for good — 3 for satisfactory?

Tom: Yes. That sort of thing. The individual scores are added up, and the total becomes the base. Next time you add the individual scores again and, if the total has gone up, the Index has gone up proportionately. Have you got it?

Martyn: I think so. Do you want me to mention the Index — and all the other things in a written report?

Tom: No need for a formal report, but I would like you to draft out a few notes to help me to prepare one. Let me know what you think the benefits are likely to be — and how you suggest we go about things. The General Manager might like us to mention the Index of Morale — and you ought to have the concept clear in your mind in case he asks you for more details.

(*Exit Martyn — trying desperately to remember all the things he has been asked to deal with.*)

Group Task

Martyn returns to his group and seeks their co-operation in producing a case in favour of the Survey which has been drafted, and generally attempts to comply with his manager's requirements.

CASE 26

Pandora's Box

San Remo (Products) Ltd.
This is a medium-sized general engineering firm (workforce 3500), which
markets a variety of products predominantly in small batches. Five months
ago the Board approved a Staff Suggestion Scheme and backed it with a
Budgetary Allocation of £4000 for a trial period of one year — £1000 per
quarter. As the Works Manager said when he put his proposal to the
Board: "This company needs ideas from the shop-floor. We've got a lot of
talents and skills and it's up to us to ensure that these aren't wasted.
Communication has got to be encouraged upwards — not just grievances.
Positive contributions are necessary."

The notification published on Staff notice-boards throughout the factory
stated *inter alia*: "If ideas of sufficient merit are not submitted in one 3
month period, the whole or part of the quarterly allocation may be carried
over to the subsequent period."

A Committee has been appointed to evaluate the suggestions submitted.
The members of this Committee include the Personnel Manager (Chairman), the Assistant Works Manager (Vice Chairman), the Senior Cost
Accountant, the Assistant Chief Engineer, and two Workers' Representatives elected to serve on the Committee by the Works Council.

The following ideas have been vetted by the Committee in their previous
meetings and adjudged worthy of final consideration for prize money. A
total of eleven ideas were put forward. The six best ones are now under
discussion:

1. Thurston Wilkie — 22 — trainee Accountant — 6 years in Accounts
   — has proposed a simple change in the invoice system which would
   mean that one copy in current use could be dispensed with. The
   Senior Cost Accountant has checked the proposals in detail and
   reckons that the annual savings would amount to approximately £300
   (£90 stationery, £210 labour).
2. Joan Maynard — 26 — Personnel Officer — joined San Remo 10
   months ago — niece of Managing Director — has suggested that the
   Selection Tests in current use could be validated. She has produced a

86

simple validation device whereby performance in four of the most common jobs in the factory could be correlated with the test scores on recruitment. The Personnel Manager has agreed to apply the proposals whatever the outcome of the Committee's deliberations.

3. Timothy Ramsbotham — 19 — Clerk in the Sales Office for past 2 years — has put forward the rather amusing idea that people in the firm might be set, or might set for themselves, Initiative Tests. He has mentioned specifically going to work in other companies to find out how they operate. Although his suggestions caused unfavourable reactions among the Committee members initially, they all admit there are possibilities here — on reflection.

4. Michael Holton — 54 — Welder in the Maintenance Department — has produced three carefully-drawn diagrams showing how the number of gas outlets in the main building can be reduced by revising the siting of pipes. The Assistant Works Manager informs the Committee that the changes suggested would be feasible and would save about £300 a year on present prices, but the costs would be in the region of £2500.

5. Colin Tracy — 16 — Apprentice Electrician — has produced a scale drawing of the existing Employee's Car Park and has shown how, by angling the spaces in one section, an extra 14 cars can be accommodated. The present capacity for employee's cars and car-parking facilities have been a bone of contention for many years. Colin's ideas have already been taken up by the Works Council and in fact an improved plan, admittedly based on Colin's, has produced space for another 24 cars.

6. Jamit Singh — 49 — Milling Machine Operator — has produced a simple coupling device which would enable the Milling Machines in his Department to be operated by certain categories of disabled workers such as Jamit's son, Jema, who used to work for San Remo but is now confined to a wheelchair as a result of a road accident. The Chief Engineer has been asked for an opinion on the device and reports that it is "ingenious, simple, and comparatively cheap to reproduce in quantity. It should be patented".

Your Assignment

Play the role of the Staff Suggestion Scheme Committee and decide how you will allocate the first quarter's Prize Money. How would your decisions be notified, and to whom?

CASE 27

"Friends, Romans, Countrymen. . . ."

Teaswell Phosphates Ltd.
The European Sales Division of the company are organising a Managers'
Conference and it is expected there will be 360 sales managers and representatives attending from sixteen different countries. For the past 4 years
the sales staff has met at a luxury hotel on the outskirts of London. The
proceedings have lasted over Thursday and Friday and the company have
footed the bills for travelling and hotel expenses. Last year the bill totalled
close on £60,000 and the Managing Director has now indicated the concern
of the board at the spiralling costs of such conferences. It has also been
mooted that there is some justifiable resentment of the part of non-sales
staff who do not get similar treatment. The non-sales staff are centred on
two large factories in the north of England.

The Managing Director has now asked the Sales Manager (Exports), in
the absence of his chief, the General Sales Manager, to report on

1. The advisability of such a conference.
2. The possibility of reducing the length and cost of the conference.

Plans for the conference are, in fact, well in advance. The General Sales
Manager is personally organising the conference this year. A proposed
skeletal agenda has already been circulated.

Thursday a.m.	Welcoming speech by Managing Director. Talk: New Products by chief Chemist.
p.m.	Film, talk and discussion: Advertising fertilisers by Market Research Manager
evening:	Dinner and Dance
Friday a.m.	Talk: Motivating Salesmen by Personnel Manager (Europe) Talk: Corporate Customers by General Sales Manager
p.m.	Open Forum: Panel includes Managing Director
evening:	Banquet

Your Assignment

Play the role of the personal assistant to the Sales Manager (Exports) who has asked you to prepare the basis for the report asked for by the Managing Director:

"An international sales force like ours need conferences like this," he says, "its a vital part of our communication system. But on the other hand we've got to consider cash flows too, and we'll obviously need to do some pruning. Let me know your thoughts."

He provides you with the following additional data (Fig. 9):

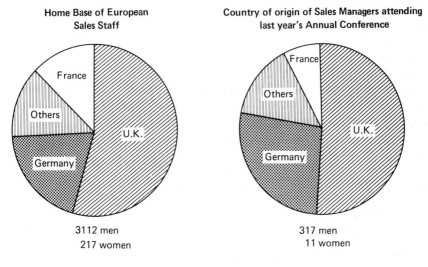

Home Base of European Sales Staff	Country of origin of Sales Managers attending last year's Annual Conference
3112 men 217 women	317 men 11 women

FIG 9

CASE 28

Silence is Golden?

Destry (Caravans) Ltd.

This company produces a range of luxury caravans, basically for the continental market. The factory is sited on the Norfolk coast and many of the workforce of 1200 were originally employed in boatbuilding on the Norfolk Broads.

In the early days industrial relations were good but recently there has been a spate of disputes. The latest trouble arose over a new bonus scheme. There were two different stoppages — the first involving all the workers in the factory for a period of six working days. The second stoppage concerned the carpenters, 76 in number, who withdrew their labour for four working days following a dispute over differentials.

A new Managing Director (Designate), Brian Blakeney, has been appointed following the early retirement of his predecessor, who became involved in a confrontation with the Board when a big contract with a firm of German distributors was recinded. The reason given by the German firm was a lack of compliance with delivery dates.

Brian diagnoses poor communications as the central problem in the business. He calls the senior executives together and explains that while he is making a journey to Germany to try to patch up the quarrel with the distributors he would like them to produce as many ideas as possible to improve the volume and quality of communications in the organisation.

"We can evaluate the suggestions when I get back", he says, "but in the meantime let's get as many ideas together as we can. The only contact we have with the workers at the moment is when there's a dispute and we run up against the Shop Steward's Committee. We don't know what their problems are, and they certainly don't understand ours. I know we need some decentralisation too — fewer levels of management acting as distortion barriers — but an organisation restructure is my problem."

Your Assignment

Play the role of Brian's team of executives. Discuss the options available and then write individual reports such as might be presented to the

90

Managing Director on his return.

Compare and evaluate the reports prepared by other members of the team.

CASE 29

Reassurance Needed

*Cromwell Insurance plc**

Melvyn Standish is sitting in his luxurious office looking out across London to the River and St. Paul's. We might expect him to be very satisfied with his lot. He is Chairman and Chief Executive of this large insurance company. The building in which he is situated is at least partly owned by the company of which he and the Trustees of his late father's estate are the major shareholders.

His father, Melvyn Standish Senior, founded the business in the 1920s with a few of his friends in the underwriting world. The company concentrated on life insurance (so-called industrial policies) in the early days. Having found this field lucrative, they turned their attention to fire-insurance overseas — particularly in the California and Florida areas in the United States. Since then the business has branched out into every aspect of insurance. Indeed, the company has recently set up a Miscellaneous Department to deal with a growing number of contracts which do not fit logically into the framework of any of the existing departments — Life — Marine — Property — Motor — Overseas — Third Party — Pension Funds — Unit Trusts.

Why should Melvyn Standish be pensive? He has on his desk a copy of the latest annual accounts — still to be published. The profits for the year are at a record level, though the results are patchy to the extent that claims in the Marine and Insurance Departments are disturbingly high.

The explanation for his discomfiture might be there on the other side of his desk, where there is a small pile of papers which are obviously absorbing him. The first document is a report from the Overseas Department covering a recent large-scale bush fire which swept through the Beverley Hills District in California. It was appreciated from the outset that the claims against the company would be very considerable. Now more details are becoming available, however, it is clear that the company will have difficulty in meeting the claims — from available liquid resources anyway. Suddenly Cromwell Insurance have got cash flow problems.

* Refer to the Companies Act 1980 to see what plc stands for. And CCC?

92

The second document is a report from a Chief Inspector whose function is to investigate complaints from clients. The following data is included:

Increases over past 12 months

Complaints over service received:	up by 12%
Complaints over complaints unattended to or inadequately attended to:	up by 38%
Complaints involving telephone conversations with members of staff:	up by 29%
Average time taken to reply to incoming mail (computed by sample):	up from 6 days to 8 days
Average time taken to settle claims (all Departments):	up from 71 days to 88 days

The Chief Inspector draws attention to the one very disturbing aspect of the situation. He gives an example of one client who had to write eleven times before a change in a schedule was accurately effected, even then only after the intervention of the Chief Inspector himself. There were many more examples which could have been given. The report concludes with the suggestion that so much of the staff's time is taken up dealing with complaints of one sort or another that they do not have sufficient time to do their normal work properly. This leads to a continuously deteriorating situation and an influx of new staff (according to the company's experience) only worsens the rate of error and puts further burdens on the existing staff. A brief survey undertaken by the Chief Inspector's staff in three Head Office Departments shows that up to 50% of staff's time is taken up in dealing with complaints — the more senior the staff the higher the proportion of time spent on these problems.

Group Discussion

What do you think is the problem here? Overstretched lines of communication? A lack of discipline? The wrong staff being employed? Inadequate induction programmes? What could be done to improve the situation? Job enrichment? How? Decentralisation? How could that be carried out?

Written Work

Produce at least two memoranda such as might have emerged as a result of Melvyn Standish's deliberations. Then exchange your memoranda with those of someone else in the group. Examine each other's work critically — but constructively.

SECTION III

Problems Centred on Personnel

Absenteeism and Lateness

More than 300 million working days are lost through certified sickness in British industry every year. A similar number of days are lost when doctors' certificates are not produced. Given a total of 21 million men and women in employment, it can be calculated that the average worker is absent from work for 28 days each year. How do we explain such a high level of absenteeism? There are a number of possible influences at work:

1. A Failure to Cater Adequately for Workers' Needs

Employees are sometimes so sick they could not possibly attend their place of work. At other times they just find an excuse to stay away. Avoidable absences such as these could be seen as a form of aggressive reaction to a frustrating work situation. Employees who find their work reasonably interesting are likely to be absent less often than those who find the job boring or stressful in some other way.

2. An Over-generous Welfare State

People are persuaded to behave in an approved fashion by a system of rewards and punishments meted out to correct *deviations* in their behaviour. Such is the sociological theory. So what sort of *incentive* is there for the worker to attend his place of work? Consider sickness benefit paid by the state. If people were to lose nothing financially when they stayed away from work — and if the work itself were unpleasant — we should not be surprised to discover high levels of absenteeism. If a man with *dependants* can claim, say, £60 a week when he does not go to work — and he earns £80 a week when he attends — this is the same as offering him 50p an hour for a 40 hour working week. How many people would work enthusiastically for 50p an hour?

3. Over-generous Employers

By the same token, some employers do little to discourage workers from

absenting themselves. Some local authorities seem to have accepted that several weeks off on sick pay is one of the perks of the job. One bus company generously wrote into their employment contracts the offer of up to six weeks sick pay if staff fell ill. In a very short time this had become an additional six weeks holiday available to all staff. Governmental circles are not unaware of the *inequity* in the situation: "Mr. Hugh Rossi, Social Security Minister said that sick pay should be taxable as many people found they were better off by being sick because their employers continue to pay them and they also claimed sick pay . . ."*

4. Affluence

Recessions apart, there is a greater preference for leisure as living standards rise. The backward bending supply curve for labour first became evident in the mid 1940s when miners who were beginning to earn high wages for the first time stayed away from work more often. They chose leisure rather than extra wages. Mondays were particularly *vulnerable.*

5. Social Acceptance of Absenteeism

In Russia and China absentees are denounced as "shirkers" and "parasites". In the West today the pressures are often in the opposite direction. Someone who works through a strike has to brave a picket line of fellow-workers hurling abuse.

Having discovered the sickness we are left to find an appropriate remedy. Perhaps like a doctor who finds his patient is suffering from terminal cancer, the medicine we prescribe is more likely to be a *palliative* rather than a cure. Mass production techniques bring material prosperity and spiritual misery. Materialism is a false god. However, for the practising manager the problems have to be dealt with in the existing *context*. For the individual firm a number of options are available:

(a) Job designs could be improved to *alleviate* boredom. Similarly, the tedium of mass production and routine, repetitive jobs could be minimised by appropriate breaks, musical accompaniment, and some form of *socialisation.*

(b) Those workers who attend regularly and punctually could be rewarded, which has the same effect as punishing the deviants. Good attendance and timekeeping bonuses are increasingly commonplace in industry.

(c) If we find out what is causing a particular problem we can apply an

*News item: Daily Telegraph — 13th February 1981

appropriate remedy. Perhaps the provision of company transport will help. Or the introduction of flexible working hours. Even the availability of a créche for young babies at the place of work might go some way to solving problems such as those we have been considering here.

Your First Assignment

Summarise the preceding passage in your own words (using a maximum of 200 words).

Your Second Assignment

Explain the meaning of the words in italics. Use a dictionary to check your answers.

Your Third Assignment

Consider the following case study. How do you think Charles Welby should deal with the problems that face him?

Case Study

Fidelity Insurance Co. Ltd.

When Charles Welby became manager of the Manchester branch of the Fidelity Insurance Company he had some strong views on how to get the best out of his staff. "Treat them considerately and they'll respond by giving their best." Noble sentiments. Most of the staff did respond positively but two of his younger staff have disappointed him.

Alison Page

Charles does not have any formal signing-on procedure, but either he or his Assistant Manager are generally around at nine o'clock to see that staff arrive punctually. If anyone arrives late persistently, Charles has a word with them. Alison has been more than ten minutes late on no less than fifteen occasions during the past month. When asked for an explanation she said she depends on her boy-friend who brings her into town in his car. They seem to run into a lot of traffic jams — and Alison's boy-friend does not have to get into work until 9.30. He works in a local accountant's office.

Her work is generally satisfactory, but Charles is concerned because she tends to be back late from lunch and is very much a "clock watcher". She is proving to be a bad influence on the other girls.

Richard Meacher

This young man is very moody. On occasions he has been rude to the Assistant Manager in front of other members of staff and Charles is aware of a personality clash between the two. Even more disturbing is the fact that a customer has recently complained about his attitude over the telephone. Richard was contrite when Charles spoke to him subsequently. It transpired that there were difficulties at home. Richard's mother and father were divorced. He had stayed with his father who was now considering remarriage. There were resulting frictions between father and son.

Richard has been having odd days off work for each of the past six weeks. He has had "a sore throat", "biliousness", "a migraine", "a tummy upset" and of course a couple of "colds".

According to the Assistant Manager, Richard's work is slightly below standard, and he is inclined to be scruffy in dress for an insurance office.

CASE 31

Top of the Pops

Jay See Plastics Ltd.

This concern produces one particular variety of plastic bottle top. It is made in three different sizes and two different colours. You represent a group of Line Supervisors called together by the Production Manager, Jim Watts. With him is the Timekeeper, Chris Fellowes, who has produced some figures on absenteeism and lateness which are now available to you. They relate to the last calendar month, in which there were 22 working days.

Absenteeism

	Average No. on payroll	Hours lost in thousands
Female operators	151	3.4
Male operators	75	1.2
Office staff (females)	15	0.2

Lateness: Late Penalties Incurred

	Morning	Afternoon
Female operators	860	64
Male operators	61	2
Office staff (females)	not applicable	

101

Analysis of Female Work-force by Age & Children

Age of mothers	Children under 14 years of age				Total
	0	1	2	3 or more	
16–25	27	16	19	3	65
26–35	10	21	34	13	78
over 35	5	2	1	0	8
					151

The present arrangement is that anyone clocking in late (other than office staff) loses half an hour's pay.

Jim Watts has been asked to put forward some ideas to the Managing Director on how absenteeism and lateness might be curbed in this situation.

Chris Fellowes has now also provided the following bar charts (Fig. 10) showing absenteeism among the different groups since the factory opened three years ago. The total number of workers has averaged about 240 during this time.

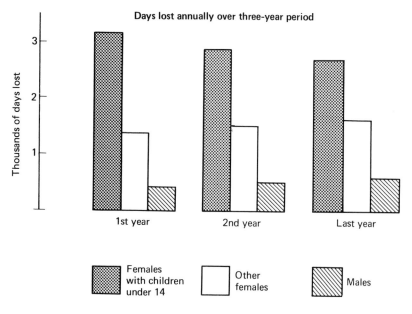

FIG 10

Your Assignment

You are asked to play the role of Jim Watts' personal assistant. He now asks you to draft a brief report on the subject such as he might be able to submit to the Managing Director. He has particularly mentioned the possibility of using (a) job rotation (b) flexible working hours and (c) a crèche for alleviating the problems. None of these are in vogue at Jay See Plastics at the present time. You may refer to the Compendium, if necessary. What other ideas would you offer?

CASE 32

Turn Again Whittington

Highlife Shoes Ltd.

Richard O'Malley moved from Leicester to London 11 years ago, and started business in a small way, making individually designed shoes in a small workshop behind his house. His wife Catherine helped generally in the business, and a small and expert group of shoemakers were soon in Richard's employ. The shoes were very exclusive and very expensive. Richard obviously had a flair for design because the volume of business continued to expand in spite of the high prices.

One day Richard was approached by the Managing Director of Centaur (Fashion Shoes) Ltd., a retail chain. Maurice Bannerman-Sanders offered him a contract which meant that Richard would be producing his shoes on a large scale — approximately 10,000 pairs a week — the shoes to be marketed through the Centaur chain under the brand name 'Trendsetter'.

The offer was so attractive Richard could not resist it, particularly as his designing talents would not be wasted. A limited company was formed, Highlife Shoes Ltd. His wife's parents bought 20% of the shoes, Maurice Bannerman-Sanders bought 40% and the remaining 40% were held in the names of Richard and Catherine. With this financial backing plus a short-term bank loan Richard took a long lease on a factory back in his native Leicester.

While Richard and Maurice concentrated on purchasing the necessary machinery and planning the layout of the factory, Catherine O'Malley undertook the task of finding the 300 of so workers of various sorts who would be required to man the new factory. The more applicants she interviews the more perturbed she becomes as she begins to appreciate that these are the people in whose hands her family's financial interests will be vested. As a result she takes her role as embryo Personnel Manager very seriously. She finds out all she can about the functioning of Personnel Departments in other organisations.

Your First Assignment

Describe briefly the functions of a Personnel Department in a typical business.

Bearing in mind the comparatively small scale of the enterprise, which of these functions would be likely to be undertaken by a Personnel Department in Highlife Shoes Ltd.

Your Second Assignment

If Catherine O'Malley decided to pass over the job of Personnel Manager, what sort of person do you think she should look for? Draw up a suitable advertisement for the post and indicate where it might appear.

An Optional Assignment

The O'Malley's appear to be doing very well in their business. However, risk and profit are often bedfellows. Can you see any particular risks for them in the present situation?

CASE 33

Take Your Pick

Britton Boatbuilders Ltd.
This company has developed an 18-foot fibre-glass auxiliary cabin cruiser which has already won a number of international awards, and it has been decided to mass produce the craft on a large scale and aim it at world markets. Market Research has been undertaken by a firm of consultants and their reports indicate that the craft should sell well in the southern coastal states in the U.S., Australia, France, Italy, and to a lesser extent Germany.

The Board appreciate the need to set up the strongest possible marketing team. Their existing Sales Manager is inexperienced in overseas selling and is going to take responsibility for the U.K. sales of the craft. He will be subordinate to a newly-appointed Sales Director (this is not to be an appointment to the Board of Directors). It is the appointment of the new Sales Director you are now asked to consider. After extensive advertising through a Personnel Consultancy, four possible candidates have emerged.

Andy Cresswell

Age 45 — married — no children — Harvard business degree — born in Charleston — still U.S. citizen — previously in U.S. Navy (12 years) and Sales Division of General Motors (5 years) — for past 3 years has been Market Research Manager (Europe) for an international oil company based in U.S. — claims to be an Anglophile having lived in London since taking up his present post — no yachting experience.

Bill Taylor

Age 52 — married — grown-up family — no academic qualifications — has a lifetime of boatbuilding experience — helped to design the craft which is now being marketed — previously owned his own yard building luxury yachts — taken over by Brittons 6 years ago — given voting shares by Brittons in payment (now holds 8% of total) — currently Chief Designer (not a member of the Board) — a regular crew member for the British entry to the Americas Cup in the early post-war years. He does not get on well with the present Sales Manager.

Walter Schultz

Age 33 — unmarried — qualified marine engineer — has recently headed a team which has succeeded in selling over a million surf-boards to Australia and the U.S. — for a German firm — followed this with a two year spell as General Manager of an American Cabin Cruiser Hire Company based on Miami — currently Advertising Manager for Rhine Boating Tours Consortium (past 12 months) — father German — mother English — speaks both languages fluently.

Tom Stott

Age 41 — married — three children aged 6 to 13 — various marketing qualifications — previously University lecturer in Marketing (5 years) — editor of Amateur Yachtsman (4 years) — currently a consultant for a top Advertising Agency (7 years) — was a Silver Medallist in Yachting in the Montreal Olympics — suffers from mild diabetes — has travelled widely in Europe during the past 18 months.

Your Assignment

Play the role of the Selection Panel and, on the evidence available, choose the most acceptable candidate from the list.

CASE 34

Limited Progress

Gellan Construction Ltd.

Jim Mathis joined the company from school 10 years ago. He had got four "O" levels but because he had been turned down for a large number of more worthwhile jobs he started as a mail clerk. He was barely satisfactory and was quickly moved on to the Filing Section. Again his stay was brief. He continued filing but was transferred to Personnel Department. His work was still regarded as mediocre, but he surprised everyone by joining classes at a local Technical College and eventually gained two distinctions in the examinations of the Institute of Personnel Management. He was given an upgrading and as a Personnel Assistant he has been "initially vetting" applications for various posts advertised by the firm in the press.

One of the company's subsidiaries has just advertised the post of Personnel Officer. The post carries a much higher salary than Jim has been earning. Jim applies for the job.

The following conversation takes place between John Fielding, Jim's boss, and Reg Kierney, the Personnel Manager of the subsidiary company:

Reg: I tried to 'phone earlier, but you were in conference. It's about this P.O.s job at Grantham. We've had an application from one of your fellows — Mathis — Jim Mathis — he's applied and frankly he's in a different class from the others. He's the best applicant by far. I'm ringing you to find out whether there's a snag. You know the job description. We want someone to interview staff for jobs — all levels up to middle rank executives — but lots of unskilled labourers too. He'd also help out devising, marking and analysing tests for various jobs. This fellow Mathis looks tailor-made for it as I say. Too good — if you know what I mean. *Is* there a snag?

John: No. Not really.

Reg: You don't sound too sure. Look, would you mind if I at least had him along for an interview.

John: No. I wouldn't have any objections.

Reg: There is one question you must answer though John. This fellow Mathis seems so overqualified for the job he's doing at the moment.

And he doesn't seem to have done any interviewing at all. I'm surprised because I know how keen you are to get all your fellows clued up on interviewing of all things. What is the explanation? Has he got a speech impediment or something? I said it before. I can sense a snag somewhere.

John: It's very difficult, Reg. Jim Mathis has got a nice personality. Maybe he's got a bit of a chip on his shoulder, but that's understandable. Jim's from the Bahamas. Well, he wasn't born there. His family came over after the war. Jim's married to an English girl — they're a nice couple. Everybody here likes him. The trouble is we have all sorts of staff to contend with. I feel it wouldn't be fair to give him interviewing work, and that's meant limiting his progress. I've tried to steer him clear of trouble. Perhaps the best thing for you is to forget about Jim Mathis for Grantham. You might be stirring up a hornet's nest. I'll tell him you've had a lot of bright boys applying for the job with more experience and so on. You leave it to me, Reg, O.K.?

Group Discussion

What are your views on this situation? How do you think the problem should be resolved?

What are the merits and limitations of anti-discriminatory legislation?

What can we do to eliminate this sort of basic injustice in our society — particularly in the workplace?

Is there any significant difference between racial and sexual discrimination related to the field of employment? (Refer to the actual Acts where possible).

CASE 35

Role Playing

"All the world's a stage,
And all the men and women merely players.
They have their exits and their entrances,
And one man in his time plays many parts."*

Man is a need-satisfying animal. Man is a frustrated animal. Man is a decision-making animal. And man is a role-playing animal.

Yes, but surely we can play the role we choose? In fact we can choose the roles we play and vary those roles only within comparatively narrow limits. There *is* an element of choice, but it can easily be exaggerated. Perhaps Timothy wants to be a policeman but he is shorter than the regulation height or has bad vision. Perhaps Sally Anne wants to be an airline hostess but has a slight stoop. These factors will limit the horizons of Timothy and Sally Anne though they might otherwise be very acceptable. Yet those who are selected to play the roles will not be allowed to vary them to any marked degree. They will be expected to behave in a pre-scribed fashion at all times. Indeed they will be sent to training schools to learn precisely what to do in a variety of situations.

Roger Brown explains:

"The word role is borrowed from the theatre. . . . A role in a play exists independently of any actor and a social role has also a reality that trancends the individual performer. . . . A social role is a set of prescriptive rules of guide to behaviour for persons of a given category. What is prescribed for the category is ordinarily performed by the category and expected from the category."†

It is important to know what to expect from those we encounter. Actions

*From *As You Like It* by William Shakespeare (1564–1616).
†From *Social Psychology*, Collier-Macmillan, 1965.

must be predictable. Hence the value of the policeman's uniform. In the words of Richard Dewey and W. J. Humber*:

> "Even though each person's behaviour is, inevitably, unique in certain ways, there are limits to which this uniqueness can be carried. In order to fit into society one must play definite and predictable roles. This ability to play constant roles must be learned."

We learn role-playing at an early age. Young children watch closely the roles that their parents play. The small boy tries to emulate his father. The small girl wants to bake cakes like her mother. As their contacts with the outside world grow they become interested in other roles. They play at being soldiers, nurses, teachers, doctors and champion sportsmen. An understanding of rights and obligations is developed. Rights are what one is entitled to expect from others, while obligations are what others are entitled to expect of us. Though we may be obliged to accept the need for playing predictable roles does this not impinge on our equally vital need to feel important as an individual regardless of the roles we play? As R. Ruddock explains†:

> "The view that all our social lives are lived in roles is unattractive for some, suggesting the imposition of uniformity on the individual. This is felt to be a threat to the supreme values of individuality, leading ultimately to alienation and dehumanisation. . . . It is not roles as such, however, that deny integrity or block the personal development of the occupant. It is particular roles that do this, while others have the opposite effect. . . . Enforced unemployment exemplifies the dangers to personality consequent on loss of roles."

Role playing is used in business and management training. In bank training schools the trainee cashiers are given a till and a supply of notes and coins. They are confronted by other trainees playing the role of customers. Cheques are presented for payment. Credits are paid into imaginary accounts. The trainee cashier becomes familiar with the role. The job obviously calls for more than the mechanical handling of money and the checking of documents. One is expected to be friendly and to

---

*From, *An Introduction to Social Psychology*. Collier-Macmillan, 1966.
†From *Roles and Relationships*. Routledge and Kegan Paul, 1969.

inspire confidence. And is mistakes are made then they can be rectified without harm during the training exercise.

Pat Armstrong and Chris Dawson explain:*

> "Role playing is a method where trainees act out the roles for which they are training or the roles of the people with whom they will interact when doing their own job. . . . Closed circuit television is often used with role playing so the trainees can review their performance and analyse their behaviour and the effect of their behaviour on others. It is then that the trainer makes his major contribution. The difficulty is that trainees may over act or "ham". Role playing is widely used in training for social skills, including industrial relations negotiation training."

When a person applies for a particular post the interviewer will be attempting to assess the candidates suitability for the role. Reference will be made to the Job Specification. What sort of qualifications are needed? What personal qualities are required? What sort of previous experience is deemed necessary? And how closely does the candidate match up to these requirements?

And for those who can play the roles best at work come the rewards. . . . the job. . . . the pay increase. . . . promotion. . . . and of course, where appropriate — the certificate or diploma.

Your Written Assignment

Express the preceding passage in your own words, limiting your abstract to a maximum of 100 words.

Case Study

Delta Department Stores Ltd.

Alec Moorhead is the Director responsible to the Board for the personal development of Senior Executives. His responsibility was established when it was realised that seven of the existing Board of Directors will reach retiring age within the next 3 years.

The Chairman commented during a Board meeting that it would be difficult to find replacements, and Alec suggested they should practise a technique which he noted being used by some companies he contacted

*From *People in Organisations*. Elms Publications, 1981.

during a recent spell of travel. The scheme involved setting up what is called a Junior Board, though this name is rather misleading since its members are high-calibre senior executives.

These executives are deemed to be potential directors.

The Chairman was not the sort to go for hare-brained schemes and asked two questions.

"What good would that do?"

"How would it operate? Briefly, mark you — briefly!"

Alec Moorhead's answers must have satisfied his Chairman because within a short space of time the Junior Board was functioning.

Your Task

Working separately, draw up a list of the pros and cons and an explanation of how the Junior Board might operate. The draft should be in a form suitable for presentation to the Chairman. When you have completed the draft, exchange it with another member of the group and criticise each other's work constructively.

CASE 36

Our Daily Bread

Wessex Granaries Ltd.
This company operates in the South and South-west of England. There are 27 different bakeries producing bread, cakes and biscuits of various types. The Head Office is on the outskirts of Bristol where the Board are now meeting to discuss the possibility of appointing additional Directors.

The existing Board consists of the Managing Director, the Sales Director (in charge of the Sales Department), the Financial Director (who is also the Chief Accountant), a Non-executive Director who has been nominated by the Holding Company to keep a watching brief on the affairs of Wessex Granaries (they hold 60% of the shares), and the Chairman who was the founder of the company and who continues to hold 20% of the equity.

The discussion has been instigated by the Holding Company who have suggested the Board could be improved by introducing some "fresh blood", though they are not putting any pressure on the Wessex Directors to make any appointments. Of their own volition the Wessex Directors have drawn up a short list of potential Board members all of whom they have vetted. They are satisfied as to the integrity of each of these candidates, and the candidates for their part have expressed a willingness to serve as Directors if invited to do so. They all have, or would be prepared to acquire, the minimum number of shares necessary for directors according to the company's Articles of Association.

The list reads as follows:

Sir Adrian Wagner — M.P. for a rural constituency — Conservative back-bencher for past 16 years — 61 years old — owns a Publishing Firm operating from Southampton — holds directorships in a Shipping Company and an Aircraft Corporation.

Geoffrey Ainsworth — Senior Partner in a Bristol law firm — owns a chain of caravan sites in Devon and Cornwall — holds Directorships in a Hotel Group, a Road Haulage Company and a Supermarket Group, all of which are local companies in the Bristol area — 52 years old.

Francis Whitbread — presently General Production Manager with Wessex Granaries — responsible for overall production in all 27 bakeries — has been with company all his working life — Directorship proposed by Chairman as a reward for his long service — 58 years old.

Paul Toombs — nominated by Managing Director who worked with him for rival company at one time — an expert in automation ('robotics') — responsible for installing £400,000 computerised production line — presently Production Manager for rivals who have one centralised bakery supplying outlying distribution units — 36 years old — a Cambridge graduate (first class honours).

Arthur Rigby — owns 40% of the shares in company which supplies Wessex with grain etc. (15% of total supplies) — brother (40%) and sister (20%) own remainder of shares — Past President of Master Millers — holds Directorships in South Wales Holiday Camps Ltd. and a local company manufacturing boiled sweets — 56 years old.

Graham Thornton — nominated by Holding Company in which he holds a non-executive Directorship — also holds Directorships in companies involved in Building and Construction (national), Supermarkets (South and Midlands), Bakery and Confectionery (Midlands) and Theatres and Cinemas (national) — regarded as an expert on all property matters — 47 years old.

Note — The Board meets every Friday at 3 p.m. In view of the growth of business it has been proposed that the Board should also meet on Tuesdays.

Your Task

Two of your number are asked to play the role of "Observers". The others are invited to act as would the Wessex Granaries' Board. At the end of the meeting, the "Observers" are invited to assess the performance of (a) the individual members and (b) the group as a whole.

CASE 37

Sixth Time Lucky

Pink Passion Products Ltd.

Scene: The pleasantly appointed office of Don Rennie, the Personnel Manager.

Players: The said Don Rennie — his secretary, Shani Lewis — and a very ruffled and agitated Production Manager, Tony Grey.

Time: The present.

Act One. Scene One.

Don is discussing a job description with Shani when Tony bursts in, unannounced. He is waving a piece of paper in his hand.

Tony: He's done it. You wouldn't believe it was possible. Here it is. Crabtree's letter of resignation. A record this time. He stayed six weeks.

(Don takes the letter and reads it to himself)

Don: I remember interviewing him when he came for the job. He seemed really keen. According to this letter, he's got a more interesting job — he didn't mention money. Poor old Tony. You're certainly unlucky with your quality-control men. This is the fifth one you've lost in a twelvemonth isn't it?

Tony: It's too bad, Don. I don't think we're getting the right sort of fellows applying for the job. Can't you make the advertisement more attractive next time so that we can have a better choice, at least.

Don: I think the trouble is we've made the job sound *too* attractive. It's a routine job — just checking the tubs. But we've got to have a qualified man in the job.

Tony: Do everything you can, Don, that's all I ask. This situation is getting ridiculous.

Don: You can't say I haven't tried. I did some calculations last time we advertised this job. We've spent £1200 on advertisements alone in the last two years.

(As Tony goes through the door, Shani brings out the Job Description)

Shani: Assistant Quality Control Manager — analyse ingredients in samples before they are used on the production line. M'm. Quite an important job. Some chemicals cause skin cancer don't they?

What advice would you offer Don Rennie and Tony Grey in this situation? Draft a suitable advertisement for them on the evidence available.

Here are three advertisements for jobs appearing in the columns of a local newspaper. Choose one of the jobs and imagine you have applied for the post and been called along for an interview. Draw up a list of six questions which you would ask the person interviewing you.

TRAINEE MANAGER/ESS
Whitecliff Hotel
A 40 bedroom 2 star hotel in the town centre. Excellent summer holiday business with varied winter programme including banquets and conferences.

Applications invited from suitable young people who are presentable, capable and willing to be trained.

Some study leave will be given.
(Apply Staff Manager)

HOSPITAL ADMINISTRATION
Clerical officer required to join a small team of Medical Records Staff in a local hospital. Applicants should be physically fit and have a cheerful understanding personality. Pay on a nationally agreed scale according to age and experience.

Apply Staff Appointments Officer,
Whitlock Hospital

CAN YOU INSPIRE CONFIDENCE
An enthusiastic sales person required in this area to sell closed circuit TV security systems to the retail trade on a top commission basis. Must have car and telephone and be capable of closing a sale.

If you are interested phone 34123

CASE 38

The Wide Open Spaces

Rio Cosmetics Ltd.

Rio Cosmetics have chosen to concentrate their effort on what they regard as the most lucrative section of the market. As their Marketing Manager says, "We've gone for short-term profit maximisation — rather than for diversification." Their production is therefore concentrated on a single tube of deodorant marketed under the brand name "Freche". The product is heavily advertised on TV and Rio have made considerable profits over the past 5 years. However, a substantial competitor has now entered the market, and Rio's share of the market has dropped to 18%, its lowest level in 3 years.

The Board are now looking for explanations. They have asked for reports from the Sales and Production Departments. They have also asked Personnel Department to report on some disturbing statistics regarding the workforce. In particular:

1. There has been a dramatic increase in absenteeism over the last year.
2. Although the number of line workers has remained fairly stable (at around 2115 during the last four or five years), weekly average output has fallen from 312,000 to 287,000 units.
3. During the last year 21% of the line workers have been late at least once a week, in spite of the fact that they lose a quarter of an hour's pay when this happens. (Before this year the figure was fairly constant at around 10%.)

In addition:

Within the past four months, the number of consumers complaining direct to the company have doubled according to the information supplied by the Quality Control Department, who keep a record of the number of letters received each week. They advise that the majority of these complaints have been traced back to what they describe as "human errors" on the production line. Furthermore, three serious cases of pilfering have been notified by the Security Section within the past week.

Other Information Available

The rate of pay is approximately 10% higher than could be obtained by the line workers elsewhere.

Older women are not discouraged, but the average age of the workforce is only 19 years. It is increasingly difficult to find acceptable line supervisors.

Production starts at 8 a.m. and finishes at 5 p.m. — 5 days a week — with an hour lunch break and two 20-minute tea breaks.

The following graphs have been prepared covering Labour Turnover and Absenteeism over the past five years (Fig.11).

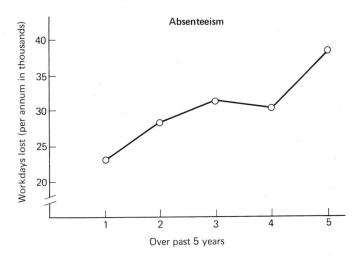

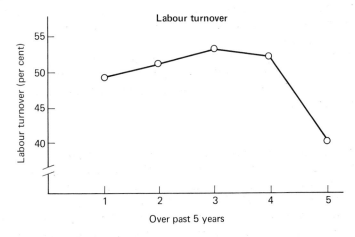

FIG 11

Your Assignment

Play the role of the personal assistant to Pat Dougan, the Personnel Manager. Offer some explanations and recommendations which might help him to produce a report for the Board of Directors.

CASE 39

Leadership

"We 'take the measure' of every man we meet. We 'size him up', or 'plot his curve', and whether or not we like to own it, to a certain extent we regulate our actions toward that one accordingly. If we judge ourselves superior, conduct takes on characteristic forms according to the occasion and our own nature: for example, haughtiness, imperiousness, condescension, the air of self importance, the instructive tone etc. On the other hand, if we judge ourselves inferior there is present a feeling of timidity, a less confident heart-beat and less steady gaze. The voice becomes hollow instead of commanding or assuring. Spoken sentences are given a rising and questioning inflection."*

Definition

Leaders may be broadly defined as those who motivate others to achieve a common goal. In a business context, the leadership role would be assumed by executives, foremen, supervisors or informal leaders of work-groups.

Function

The leader's function is to achieve results through other people, and in order to do this he must have the ability to persuade people to do the work. The behaviour of the workforce has to be influenced towards the achievement of certain prescribed goals or objectives.

The study of leadership assumes importance because an effective leader will produce better results than an ineffective leader and these results, in terms of productivity, will benefit (*prima facie*) the nation, the business owners, the employees, and society generally. Productivity is broadly

---

*From an article by L. M. Terman, A preliminary study of the psychology and pedagogy of leadership *Journal of Genetic Psychology*, 1904.

121

correlated with profits. More profits mean a larger wage fund available to the workers and a larger potential dividend for the shareholders. The Government will benefit from the increased taxes paid. Much of the Government's spending will be on welfare of one sort or another. Hence the spread of benefits suggested here, and the importance of the subject to us all.

So how can we improve the effectiveness of managers?

1. We can train them in mechanistic techniques such as costing, account-ing and computer technology. Managers must be numerate.
2. We can give them an increased understanding of the human beings who make up the workforce. A chemist is expected to know the effect of adding one volatile substance to another. An engineer will know the stresses and strains which can be borne by particular metals. So, since managers by definition deal with people, they should under-stand the propensities of their workforce.
3. We can give the managers experience in decision-making. In the early stages of their careers they can be taught to cope with the routine and comparatively minor problems which arise in any business. And as they climb the ladder they can learn to face the more complex and challenging problems. The important point to note is that the pro-gression is planned and is not haphazard.
4. We can attempt to find, at an early stage in their business careers, those people who have leadership potential, so we can ensure their capabilities are fully developed and utilised.
5. We can encourage the managerial style which is most effective. The range of possible leadership styles is shown in Table 1.

There is no leadership style which suits all situations. As Pat Armstrong and Chris Dawson point out:*

> "In a highly structured situation such as an operating theatre, or in a battle, an authoritarian leader may be required, whereas in a very loosely structured situation a more democratic style might lead to more effective performance."

However, we are moving towards an industrial democracy, albeit slowly and painfully. Workers' expectations have changed and are continuing to change. So it is not surprising to find the participative style of

---

*From *People in Organisations*, Elms Publications, 1981.

Table 1 *Range and Features of Leadership Styles*

Leader-centred (Autocratic)	Group-centred		Individual-centred ("Free rein")
	Participatory	Democratic	
1. Leader makes all final decisions for the group without consultation.	1. Leader makes decisions after consultation with group.	1. Decisions made by the group (majority vote).	1. Leader gives no suggestion for problem-solving.
2. Close supervision.	2. Increased communication between leader and members.	2. Voting based on the principle of one man — one vote.	2. Each individual acts according to his own dictates within widely defined limits.
3. Individual members praised and criticised publicly.	3. Leader is supportive i.e. considerate.	3. All members bound by the group decision.	3. A lack of co-ordination and control.
4. Subordinates treated without respect for their feelings.	4. Leader is accessible for consultation with individuals.	4. All members may contribute to discussion.	
5. More demanded than can be reasonably done.	5. Questioning approach encouraged.	5. Development of coalitions and cliques.	
6. Questioning discouraged except to clarify instructions.	6. Modus operandi largely unspecified.	6. Leadership role is assumed by Chairman.	

leadership is generally likely to be most effective. Robert C. Appleby explains:*

> "A less authoritarian style of leadership has been shown to reduce conflicts from the workers' resentment of the power of managers. Where managers are pleasant and co-operative and acknowledge feelings of others conflict is reduced. There is also an idea to institute structural changes to *reduce* the amount of supervision a worker is subjected to and give him a greater control over his own."

The words of John Gardner should be comforting to those students who aspire to managerial posts and are acquiring social skills through training in group discussions and co-operative tasks. He believes that:†

*From *Modern Business Administration*, Pitman Publishing, Second Edition, 1976.
†From *The Observer*, 26 November, 1978.

"The most effective leadership will be provided by an individual, or better yet, a closely-linked group of individuals with:

   (i) The patience to work in a context of complexity and pluralism;

  (ii) The intellectual clarity to conceptualise a working consensus;

 (iii) The integrity to win the trust of contending forces;

 (iv) The persuasiveness to mobilise willing allies in pursuit of goals that are tolerable for all.

     . . . There are many young people with the ability, temperament and inclination to reach strategic positions. . . . Society's task is to identify them early and provide them with experiences that will strengthen them for the work they must do. . . . One fundamental outranks all others: they must be exposed to experiences that broaden their horizons, lift them out of their specialities, introduce them to other worlds and other views."

Your First Task

Make an abstract of the preceding narrative, limiting yourself to a maximum of 120 words.

Case Study

Trikota Banking Corp.

Monday, February 18th

Dan Davis, newly-appointed General Manager, has his first meeting with his Senior Executives. He soon learns that Joe Brent (Manager–Advances) feels very strongly about the poor-quality staff allocated to his department.

Tony Wood (Manager-Personnel) defends the selection process he has been using, and indicates he has taken extra special care over recruitment for and transfer to the Advances Department since the latest series of complaints from Brent.

"I appreciate you need high quality staff to vet the applications for the more substantial loans and overdrafts," he says.

"Well, things don't get any better," says Brent," I don't blame Personnel, but there aren't many of these fellows who would have made cashier when I joined the bank. Analysts for Advances! Psssh!" Dan Davis is grateful when this particular disagreement dies down so that the meeting can get on with more important matters. Last year's profits were below the target set by the Holding Company and Dan's brief is to ensure that this year's slightly more modest target is met.

Wednesday, February 27th

John Young is an Economics graduate. He joined Trikota Banking Corporation 18 months ago, since when he has been gaining varied experience in one of the larger banking branches. He is talking to one of his non-banking friends in the "Duke of Bedford" over a pint of larger.

"I only heard yesterday. I'm quite looking forward to working in London — for a spell anyway. They told me when I joined they would be giving me responsibility within 2 years, and they've kept their word. I must say there've been times when I wondered whether I did the right thing going into banking — but this job in Advances Department seems just what I'm looking for. I got this message to go up to Head Office — saw the Personnel Manager — a fellow called Wood — interviewed me when I first joined. Another five hundred a year — and the sky's the limit! Have another one?"

Friday, March 8th

Joe Brent is on the telephone in his office.

"Yes, I am *am* still overworked! I've been without a P.A. for 3 weeks now. What's that? — Oh him! He just didn't have a clue. He gave in his notice after 6 weeks. I've got someone else coming on Monday. Tony Wood says he's the cat's whiskers, but he said the same about the last one. Another College boy. Still wet behind the ears. I've never had a good one yet."

Your Assignment

You are Mr. Davis' personal assistant.

"I think Brent ought to give his new staff a formal induction programme when they join him," he confides, "I also think he needs reminding that staff turnover is expensive. Draft me a short note for him will you. He seems as prickly as a hedgehog so for goodness sake be diplomatic. . . . Oh yes, and I see there's a Human Relations Course for Senior Management on the 19th of next month. . . . at the bank training school. At least I can suggest he might like to attend. It's only for the day, and quite a lot of the senior branch managers will be attending."

CASE 40

The Whiz Kid

Alpha Tours Ltd.

This company has built up an excellent reputation among its clients over the past two decades. The tours it offers are linked with first-class accommodation in carefully selected hotels. Alpha coaches are luxurious and include bar and buffet facilities. Experienced and well-paid Guides are provided to ensure that the tourists enjoy every possible facility. The company prides itself in the fact that so many of its clients make subsequent bookings. The clients are encouraged to do so by Alpha's generous 10% reduction for any bookings in successive years.

The General Manager has recently retired and his replacement is Brian Kydd who was recruited from outside the company. He is now putting forward his suggestions for changing Alpha's "outdated" policies. Epitomised, his plans could be expressed thus:

1. An economy campaign aimed at increasing profits by pruning expenditure while holding prices constant.
2. Providing extra seating on the coaches by removing the buffet bars and introducing retractable "lap tables" for each individual passenger.
3. The use of good-class hotels rather than exclusively first-class hotels.
4. A new grade of Guide to be employed using carefully selected students for this purpose. Some tours to dispense with Guides altogether.
5. A reduced allowance in the budget for coach maintenance and repairs — the new General Manager finds this is currently 50% higher per coach than was allowed in his previous company.

Your Task

Play the role of Mr. Kydd's personal assistant who has been asked to suggest how these new policies might be introduced. Your proposals should be in writing and should bear in mind the effect the changes might have on (a) staff and (b) customers.

When the proposals have been committed to paper you are then invited
to exchange your work with that of one of the other members of your
group. Read through each other's work and comment critically — and
constructively.

CASE 41

Unit Five

Gamma Furniture Ltd.
This company grew out of a one-man business established by Louis Steiner at the turn of the century. Even between the Wars (1918–1939) the business was operating on a comparatively small scale, with Louis, his two sons, and a handful of workers producing hand-made furniture of high quality.

Louis died during the early post-war period and his son Morris took over the reins. His first step was to form a limited company. Next, he borrowed heavily from the bank, using as security:

1. the assets of the new company, and
2. the personal guarantee of his brother-in-law.

He was then able to sell the rather small workshop in which his father had started the business, and buy a modern factory on the outskirts of London. The company prospered sufficiently to go public in the early 1960s, Morris and his immediate family retaining approximately 40% of the voting shares.

At this stage, when everything seemed well set, there was a period of disappointment. The company found itself in the doldrums largely as a result of rising costs of production and intensive competition. For three successive years profits were insufficient to warrant payment of a dividend. But Morris demonstrated his business acumen by discovering a talented young designer on his staff who was able to change the fortunes of the firm. Danny Schaffer produced a succession of very distinctive and highly successful designs for interlocking furniture units which found a ready market. These were sold under the description of Unit Five Furniture.

Gamma became revitalised. The demand for Unit Five Furniture was so great that a new factory was opened up at Reading 2 years ago, and another is in course of construction on the outskirts of Bristol. All this is history. This morning Danny Schaffer has sought an audience with Morris Steiner.

"I'm going into business on my own," he tells his boss. "I've been able to put my hands on a bit of capital and I want to try a few ideas out for myself."

Morris ponders. He has never failed to appreciate Danny's value to the firm and his loss could be a blow to Gamma's plans for expansion.

Questions for the Group

1. How do you think Morris might have dealt with this predicament?
2. How would the following groups be affected by Danny Schaffer's departure from Gamma?
   (i) the shareholders (ii) the directors
   (iii) the workpeople (iv) the customers.
3. What relevance would patents have to these issues. Using the resources of your college library find out all you can about the Law of Patents.
4. How does the graph in Fig. 12 help to provide Morris with useful information? These are the latest available figures.

FIG 12

Assignment

At the end of the discussion complete a Report Form and compare it with the suggestions in the Guidelines.

CASE 42

An Immovable Object

Hoxa Holdings Ltd.

You are the Directors of the Holding Company. There are two subsidiaries and their annual accounts are now under scrutiny. The companies are of comparable size and are both producing different components for the Motor industry. Apex's works are situated on the outskirts of Liverpool, while Bertwell's factory is to the south of Oxford. The figures below are extracted from the accounts to the 31st. December last and records provided by the Personnel Department:

	Apex Ltd.	*Bertwell Ltd.*
Capital invested in the business (£ million)	13	12
Net profit for year (£ million)	1.7	0.5
Average working-force during year ('000s)	14.1	13.1
Days lost through strikes ('000s)	37	41
Labour turnover (per annum)	12%	17%
Absenteeism — days lost ('000s)	74	92
Annual wages bill (£ million)	83	81

The Managing Director of Apex Ltd. is Chris Amber — 45 years old. He has instituted an apparently effective system of Management by Objectives. He is also applying Job Enrichment techniques in selected areas of his plant. Early reports are encouraging.

The Managing Director of Bertwell is Charles Bertwell — 59 years old. He is a member of the founding family who still hold 51% of the equity between them. He is known to be against what he refers to the "new approach".

You now have to consider how to deal with this situation. Appoint a Chairman and act as a Board of Directors would. You can assume that neither Chris Amber nor Charles Bertwell are present.

Problems Centred on Industrial Relations

CASE 43

Them v. Us

Industrial relations in Britain have been established mainly on a voluntary basis, although there is a considerable volume of legislation covering the conditions of employment and the rights of individual employees.

"Both employers and employees are free to form voluntary associations and to negotiate with each other. The State is ready to provide assistance where the organisation of workers, employers, or both, is inadequate to conduct negotiations, or where the usual methods of resolving disagreements have failed."*

In spite of the attempts to encourage conciliation and common purpose, there is an obvious polarisation of attitudes and loyalties in large sections of British industry. The distinction between "management" and "worker" is well understood, even if the dividing line is blurred in practice. Of course attitudes vary.

"Workers' attitudes — like the attitudes of any other group — are not formed overnight. They depend not only on past experience, but on parental influence, historical background, the traditions of an industry and even on geographical location. A workers' attitude towards his management will also vary from one sector of industry to another. In an industry like brewing, where units have always been small and where there are strong family traditions, attitudes will be likely to differ from those in, say, shipbuilding, where units are large and communications stretched. Against this background, management is not 'Mr. John', a familiar figure in the brewery, but someone more remote, seen as the representative of the directors who are still more remote."†

*Pamphlet on Industrial Relations, Central Office of Information, HMSO, 1977.
†Marjorie Caton Jones, *Industrial Disruption*, Ed. C. Northcote Parkinson. Leviathan House, 1973.

Even the nature of the problem is perceived differently by those who are seeking acceptable solutions. There are those who see all those involved in the organisation as members of a team, striving with a common purpose towards a mutual goal. This is what has become known as the "Unitary" frame of reference.

> "How do managers holding a unitary frame of reference explain the existence of conflicts? Quite simply they only have two answers available to them. Firstly (and quite commonly nowadays), they put it down to poor communications. In doing this they accept some of the responsibility for the conflict. What they say is, 'If only we had been able to communicate better with our workers, then they would have understood that what we intended to do, or have done, is for their benefit.' Or to put it another way, the whole conflict is the result of a most unfortunate misunderstanding.
> "The second explanation is less generous. This runs along the lines that the management has done all it possibly could to show the workers that the course of action proposed, or taken, is the right one for the organisation (and, therefore, also the workers), but that this has been rejected because of the action of a handful of militant, extremist agitators who, by devious means, have managed to mislead the general workforce."*

So what is the contrary view to the "unitary" concept of industry? It is known as the "pluralistic" frame of reference. Any enterprise contains groups of people with widely varying interests and aspirations. Sometimes the interests of the different interests coincide; often they do not.

> "Given such views conflict is not abnormal, but is to be expected. Management and governments should not expect blind obedience, nor try to suppress any ideas or aims which conflict with their own; their aim rather should be to try to reconcile conflicting opinions and keep the conflict within accepted bounds so that it does not destroy the enterprise altogether."†

Workers' attitudes also differ in other industrial societies. For example, the Japanese have a reputation for endeavour, efficiency and industrial harmony. Anthony Bambridge's report from Tokyo made interesting read-

*Pat Armstrong and Chris Dawson, *People in Organisations*. Elms Publications, 1981.
†Ibid.

ing for a Briton attuned to very different expectations. Picture the scene as the men and women of Matsushita Electric clock on and join together to sing the company song before they start the day's work:

"For the building of a new Japan
Let's put our strength and minds together,
Doing our best to promote production
Sending our goods to the people of the world,
Endlessly and continuously,
Like water gushing from a fountain.
Grow industry, grow, grow, grow.
Harmony and sincerity!
Matsushita Electric!

"In Japan it is the group that matters, never the individual. . . . Life is a matter of 'us' against the outside world. . . . In return for his loyalty to a leader the subordinate will expect to be consulted on all major issues. . . . Decision-making is a painfully slow process and is always by consensus. Once a course of action is approved, however, everyone in the company is identified with it and backs it with all their energy."*

Anthony Bambridge's impressions were reinforced a few years later by Eldon Griffiths on a visit to Toyota city:

"The third reason why Japanese industry is outstripping ours is better labour relations. The main source of this is a spirit of company loyalty. There is far less 'them' and 'us' in Japanese industry. The shopfloor feels itself to be part of the same team as the boardroom. At Toyota I was impressed by an atmosphere very similar to that which one still finds in those family firms where the proprietor accepts a personal responsibility for his employees' welfare. Few Toyota workers are ever sacked. In return they expect — and are expected to give their best to the job. Deep down they believe that what is good for Toyota is also good for them!"†

More recently Koji Nakamura was able to add further to our understanding of the great gulf in attitudes to the work situation between Japan and Britain:

*The Observer, 15 April 1973.
†The Daily Telegraph, 18 November 1975.

"Labour mobility in Japan is far less than in other industrial countries, primarily because of the employees' loyalty to the company, sustained largely by a life-time employment system. It is partly because of this system that employees are organised into corporate rather than craft unions. This breeds a feeling of being on board the same ship as the employers, a feeling of 'family identity and membership' rather than of 'class confrontation'."†

Perhaps, in fairness, it should be pointed out that in Japan there is no Welfare State as exists in Britain. This forces the Japanese worker to depend more on his employer. No doubt increasing affluence and the passage of time will bring about changes of attitude in the new generations of Japanese workers, but influences can work in both directions. Peter Hazelhurst, writing from Tokyo provided us with an example. A seminar was being addressed by Mr. Hiroshi Okochi, the director of the Sony Corporation's operations in Europe, who was explaining the secrets of the successful operations in their plant at Bridgend:

"When we first decided to set up the venture in the United Kingdom we had to ask ourselves: what conditions encourage industrial unrest? If workers are treated with inequality, they will inevitably stage strikes. That was the conclusion," he said.

"The first step was simple. Shortly after Sony took over its Bridgend plant three years ago, the Japanese directors tore down partitions which divided managerial staff from workers in the plant's cafeteria. After stiff resistance, the British managerial staff and the technicians were also persuaded to adopt Japanese customs and wear the same uniforms as the production line workers.

"The British managerial staff, who were trained in Japan, were also encouraged to follow the example of their Japanese counterparts, who meet their subordinates over a drink after work to form a closer relationship between management and labour ... This has proved extremely useful in promoting a good atmosphere and communications between the two sectors," he said.*

In Europe the movement towards industrial democracy has been concentrated on devices such as Works Councils and worker represen-

†*The Times*, 18 December 1980.
The Times, 15 November 1976.

tation on the Board of Directors. In Britain, the developments have been more fragmented, and worker representation has remained the prerogative of Trade Unions and Shop Stewards, who have tended to see Management as the "enemy". We may chuckle at the thought of Japanese workers singing the company song before they start work. But no doubt they chuckle at us, fighting amongst ourselves, instead of getting on with the job of producing the cars, the television sets and the houses which our people need.

Group Discussion

What are your views on this? How do you see the *future* of industrial relations in Britain? How do you see the needs of Japanese workers catered for, at each level, in terms of Maslow's Hierarchy of Needs?

Written Assignment

Make an Abstract of the preceding narrative using a maximum of 150 words.

Case Study

Denton Autos Ltd.

Denton Autos produce one car — the D.A. Sports Special — a fast luxury two-seater. There are some 2500 workers who are represented by twelve different Unions. Industrial relations have been above average for the motor industry, and the Works Manager, Ray Stevens, reckons part of the explanation lies in the special Cost of Living Index developed in co-operation with the Combined Union Committee. This coupled with a Wages Fund which gives the workers 50% of the trading surplus distributed in accord with the directions of the Committee. As a result of these special features, workers at Dentons have tended to earn 5–15% higher wages than similar workers elsewhere.

You are asked to play the role of the Shop Stewards Committee which is meeting to consider the following problems which have arisen during the course of the last few days:

1. A night shift worker, Bernard Duffy, was found sleeping behind one of the store-rooms at 4.30 a.m. The Supervisor reported the matter to Ray Stevens who has sacked him "on the spot". A member of the Committee has spoken to Duffy who says it is common practice to "get your head down when you've done what you're supposed to". He claims that others were doing the same thing and were disre-

garded by the other supervisors. The Supervisor who reported Duffy was new to the night shift.

2. Security Guards posted at the main entrance carried out some spot checks on workers leaving the factory yesterday evening. The Chief Security Officer has authority from Management to make such checks as he feels are necessary, but last evening 36 workers were subjected to a full search. Two workers were found to be carrying company equipment on their person. One man had a heavy duty torch in his denims. He used this in his work on the assembly line. The other was found to be carrying a dismantled electric spot welder in his brief case. It is not known yet what action will be taken.

3. Management have suggested that a new system of group working should be introduced. Details are not available yet, but it is clear that the old assembly lines would be scrapped and cars would be made from start to finish by small "teams" of workers. The Works Manager has intimated that the Committee would be invited to participate in the development of the new system. At this stage, however, they are simply asked to signify their willingness to co-operate with the Management's Work Study team.

4. Information has been given to the Chief Shop Steward concerning the Company's Interim Accounts. For the first time, the company are reporting a loss (reputedly £100,000) which is being blamed on a falling share in the American market — through encroachment by two new Japanese models, and the last wage increases.

5. A new car park has been laid out in newly-acquired land adjacent to the factory. Management originally agreed that this should be for the exclusive use of the workers, but they are now claiming 36 spaces in the old car park — "for executives and customers".

Your Assignment

After group discussion, you are invited to notify the Works Manager of the Committee's responses to these items of news. Your response should take the form of a written report collectively approved.

CASE 44

In the Moonlight

The National Health Service
The Atherdene District Management Team are responsible for the administration of a group of seven different hospitals in their area. They meet regularly to discuss problems arising and on the agenda today are two matters to do with staff in which the Authority are involved with the National Union of Public Employees. The nature of the first problem is evidenced by the memorandum from the Catering Manager at Frensham County Hospital. This has been passed on to the Management Team by the Section Administrator (Personnel).

Atherdene District Health Authority
Memorandum

To: Marion Powell
    Section Administrator (Personnel)

From: Richard Cotsworth
    Catering Manager
    Frensham County

Re Mrs. Helen Coombes — Catering Assistant

Mrs. Coombes joined my staff 18 months ago and has been a satisfactory worker generally although she has been absent for a total of 53 days — for only 10 of which was a medical certificate forthcoming. Last week she was absent on Monday and Tuesday. When she returned she reported that she had been suffering from a 'severe migraine'. This condition has been used to explain previous absences. However, on Monday evening my senior Supervisor, Mrs. V. Bishop, had reason to visit the Valkyrie Club in the High Street here, and spotted Mrs. Coombes working in the back room preparing sandwiches. When I confronted Mrs. Coombes with this information at 8.30 am on Wednesday morning she denied it initially but eventually admitted that she had been doing this work at the Valkyrie for the past four months. She said that her migraine had disappeared on Monday evening, but had returned by the time she woke up on Tuesday morning.

I am not satisfied with this story and I am asking that the authority send Mrs. Coombes an official warning that this sort of thing will not be tolerated. It has an adverse effect on other staff. If this happens again I recommend that she be sacked.

R Cotsworth,

21st August 1983.

The other side to the story, and the details of a second problem, emerge in the letter from NUPE which is reproduced below.

NATIONAL UNION OF PUBLIC EMPLOYEES

No. 5 Area Office,
Portland Court,
Atherdene.
28th August 1983.

The District Administrator
Atherdene District Health Authority,
Wellington House,
Atherdene.

Dear Sir,
It has come to my notice that one of my members, Mrs. Helen Coombes, a catering assistant at Frensham County Hospital, has been threatened with dismissal. The complaint by the catering manager at the hospital is that she was seen working in a local club. The first point I would make is that there is nothing in Mrs. Coombes' contract of employment which denies her the right to take on another job in the evenings if she so wishes. The second point I would draw your attention to is Mrs. Coombes present domestic difficulties. She has the unenviable task of bringing up a six-year-old daughter without the benefit of a male breadwinner. It is surely a reflection on the low rates of pay earned by catering staff in the Health Service that

Mrs. Coombes is obliged to take on additional evening work in order to make ends meet!

While writing to you there is one other matter which has come to my attention. Discussions are apparently taking place in the Authority to use young school leavers to cover staff absences during future holiday periods. My Union would certainly like to be consulted before any commitments are made. There are important principles at issue here. Of course some young people can be given employment in various departments within the service, but we are looking for permanent full-time posts. We do not want to see these young people exploited as a source of cheap labour and at the expense of our members.

Yours faithfully,

P Short

NUPE Area Officer

Your First Assignment

Discuss these problems together. How do you think the District Management Team should cope with these issues? What attitude do you think the Union officials should adopt? What steps could be taken generally to reduce the number of school leavers who do not find jobs?

Your Second Assignment

Using the facilities in your college library and working as a team, find out all you can about the legal requirements before an employee can be dismissed. Then write an appropriate memorandum from the Section Administrator (Personnel) to the Catering Manager at Frensham County Hospital. You may assume that the District Management Team have agreed to support the Catering Manager.

CASE 45

"If You Can't Beat Them — Join Them!"

Apex Manufacturing Co. Ltd.

Industrial relations in this firm have been abysmal. Over the past 5 years, days lost through strike action have been double the national average. Furthermore, the level of output has been so low that the company has not made a profit in the last three annual accounts. Peter Trenchard, the Managing Director, has been exploring various methods of improving the relationship between management and workers. He was appointed 3 months ago on the strength of his success in dealing with a similar situation in another company in the group.

Trenchard favours offering a seat on the board to a nominee of the branch of the principal Trade Union involved in production. John Graham, the Chairman, is aghast when the suggestion is made at a board meeting. Together with his father, now retired, and his married sister, he owns 30% of the voting shares. He is not involved with the day-to-day administration of the company, but has strong opinions on how it should be run. Two other non-executive directors share his disapproval. Graham agrees that some action is called for, but prefers the notion of offering the workers shares in the company. However, Trenchard does have one valuable ally:

"I think we should listen carefully to what Mr. Trenchard has to say," says Robin Delage, who is the Holding Company's nominee on the Board. "Things cannot be worse than they are. We are trying to avoid a complete close-down."

"Of course we'll listen, but there are so many arguments against the idea."

"Well, Mr. Trenchard?" says Delage while the remaining directors wait expectantly.

Your Assignment

Discuss the issues involved here. Then complete a Report Form evaluating the proposals.

Ammunition for the Discussion

An article in the Sunday Times of the 2nd August 1981 by Joe Irving told of a militant Shop Steward who had become a shareholder in the engineering company he works for. He was still a staunch trade unionist but was among the first to join the company's share option scheme. The article went on to explain:

"Schemes enabling selected employees — usually directors or executives — to share in profits have been around for a number of years. What is new about the schemes set up under the 1980 Finance Act is that all employees have a right to join.

"An option scheme allows them to buy shares at a future date at a pre-determined price. To pay for the shares, employees must first save the money in the government's Save As You Earn or an equivalent building society 'Sharesave' scheme.

"An agreed amount is deducted from pay every month for five years. At the end of the period, there will be the right amount of cash to pay for the required number of shares at today's price, with a discount of up to 10%.

"In the meantime, there is a good chance, that the shares will have risen to produce a good profit. If not, you can forego the option and withdraw your savings."

On Trenchard's side, it can be pointed out that in most E.E.C. countries large companies now have two tiers of directors. The Supervisory Board at the apex has strong worker representation (in Germany, for example, 50% of the directors on the Supervisory Board are elected by the workers). In Britain, the Post Office has experimented with the appointment of Worker Direcors to various Area Boards. Many of the arguments for Worker Directors are set out in the Bullock Report.

CASE 46

The Magna Carta

Jenson & Co. Ltd.

Jensons manufacture furniture. Their factory is on the outskirts of a market town in the West Midlands. They make high-quality reproduction furniture, mainly hi-fi units, coffee tables and wall units. Pete Grimshaw has called a meeting of his top executives. He is Works Manager of Jensons and has been briefed by his Board to prepare a Constitution for a new Works Council. The only firm instructions so far are that the Council will meet in the Works Canteen on the third Wednesday of every month, and shall be given "a reasonable amount of decision-making power in the area of responsibility normally reserved for the Works Manager".

Eddie Lambert, one of the few line managers with any experience of Works Councils (in a previous job) gets involved in a difference of opinion with Len Purcell, the Personnel Manager:

Eddie: I don't think much of Works Councils. The more power you give them the more they want. We even had them in on discussions for bonus schemes. They ended up voting themselves more money.

Len: I don't agree with that — but times are changing. Workpeople expect to be told more. They expect to be involved. Works Councils are obligatory elsewhere in the E.E.C. for companies like ours.

Eddie: I still think it's better to deal with the Unions direct. The Works Council's just a talking shop.

Len: By all means talk to the Unions too. We've got our Joint Consultation Committee. But what about the 35% of our workers who don't belong to a Union?

Pete reminds them that the Board have given them the O.K. and the task now is to draw up a meaningful Constitution.

Your Assignment

It is going to take a lot of spadework before Jensons produce a Constitution for a Works Council, but you are invited to specify six points — the most important six in your view. For example, you may wish to refer to the number of Workers' Representatives to be elected, and to the method of election. What sort of matters will be considered? What matters will be outside the province of the Council? What voting procedures will there be? Will there be veto powers? The Management Representatives on the Council have already been chosen: the Works Manager (or his deputy), the Personnel Manager and Eddie Lambert.

Finally, draw up a list of the likely merits and demerits of a Works Council such as is being proposed here.

Details of the workforce (excluding Managers):

	Foremen/Supervisors		Workers	
	(Male)	(Female)	(Male)	(Female)
Machine Shop	5	-	42	-
Assembly Line 1	13	6	61	102
Assembly Line 2	7	12	51	114
Assembly Line 3	21	5	86	139
Store	3	8	29	7
Despatch Department	5	-	23	-
Polishing Bay	5	-	29	23
Spraying Shop	5	-	27	-
Inspection Section	7	-	23	-
Repairs Section	2	-	18	5
Transport Section	3	-	31	-
Office	3	8	9	48
Canteen	-	3	2	17
	79	42	431	455

In addition there is an all-male Sales Department, located in offices 5 miles from the factory. The staff there consists of 27 Sales Representatives who are generally out touring the country.

CASE 47

Double or Quits

The Southern Belle
Two daily newspapers in the Manston Group are being amalgamated in order to combat rising costs and falling circulation and advertising revenue.

The Southern Star

This paper sells mainly in the Southern Counties. The average daily circulation over the last six months has been 156,000. General layout — two pages for national news — six pages for local news (divided into three different editions for different geographical areas) — two pages for features — remainder for advertisements.

> Printing staff: 196 (26 female).
> News and Office staff: 36 (12 female).
> Printing Works and offices at Winchester.

The Morning News

This paper concentrates on national news — six to eight pages — with two pages devoted to local items for the area of circulation — the Southeast including London. The average daily circulation over the last 6 months has been 362,000.

> Printing staff: 284 (63 female of whom 29 are married to males employed in the Printing Works).
> News and Office staff: 49 (37 female).
> The Printing Works are at Bow while the Editorial staff have offices at Finchley.

Note: There is a Closed Shop policy operated in connection with both newspapers.

The Southern Belle

This is the completely new paper which is to be published. A Market Research Agency has studied the market and as a result of their report, the Manston Board have decided to publish a different sort of daily newspaper. It is believed that the public want to absorb the news through the television media, so the Southern Belle is going to concentrate on features — particularly those of general interest to the family. The Market Research Agency have discovered that there is a marked tendency for papers to stay in the house and to be read by the female members of the family. The Daily Clarion is to be designed accordingly. It is hoped to keep the circulation around the half-million mark — 400,000 will be the estimated break-even point. A printing staff of 250 (50 female) will be required together with an editorial staff of 45 (20 female).

The Printing Works at Bow have already been sold to developers though they will not be taking possession for some time. The Offices at Finchley are to be taken over eventually by another company in the Manston Group.

The Southern Belle will be produced from the Winchester Works and Offices, which will be slightly enlarged to accommodate the extra staff.

Your Assignment

Consider the following questions together. Then sketch out some recommendations for the Manston Board with regard to the pending changes.

What staff problems are likely to be encountered?

What sort of resistance to the changes would you expect? Why?

What role do you think the Unions could be expected to play in this amalgamation?

What steps would you recommend, bearing in mind that the staff have not yet been notified of the amalgamation?

CASE 48

The Residuary Legatee

Joshua Bull Ltd.

Orlando Behling is an American. He has recently graduated from New York University (majoring in Psychology). He has been over to England a few times and regards you as his friend and confidante. While over in England, he met his elderly Uncle Joshua (his mother's eldest brother) and he obviously made quite an impression. A few weeks ago Joshua died and it now transpires that he has left the residue of his estate — including his 51% of the voting shares in the company he founded — to Orlando — his only surviving male relative.

He is coming over to England again later on but has asked you to look after things for him in the meantime. As a first step you visit the solicitor handling the estate:

> "It's quite a big concern by all accounts," he tells you. "The shares have been provisionally valued at £250,000, though there'll be quite a bit of estate duty to pay. But I understand the company hasn't made any profits for the past couple of years. All those are problems which will sort themselves out in the end, but you've got an immediate problem. I've had the Chief Executive on the 'phone within the last hour and it appears he is taking another post. Joshua knew all about it apparently but doesn't seem to have taken any action."

It seems that Joshua was a bit of a law unto himself and although there were three other directors he was very much the dominant character. However, you decide to visit the works — in a northern industrial town — and meet the Chief Executive who is obviously determined to leave within the coming weeks. He tells you of the latest crisis. There is to be a confrontation with the Shop Stewards Committee on the morrow. In brief, they are demanding:

1. Management action in regard to a recent National Wages Agreement which has raised the Standard Rate by 10 pence per hour. The Committee are claiming that the rate for Bull's workers should be

increased by 12 pence per hour because they have always enjoyed 20% more than the National Rate.

2. Immediate Management action with regard to machine guards for certain machines. A recent accident resulted in serious injury to one of the Machine Operators. The Committee are insisting that special guards be attached to the offending machines although there is apparently no legal obligation. (The Chief Executive informs you there are six machines and the cost of the guards would be about £400 each.)

3. The Committee have previously accepted that 150 workers will need to be made redundant during the course of the next six months as a result of the introduction of a new fully-computerised production line. The Committee use the term "robots". Management have asked for the right to select which workers are to be retained, but the Committee are insisting on the principle of "last in-first out".

The Chief Executive explains that he is prepared to take instructions but he is committed to take up his new appointment at the end of next month.

Your Assignment

First, discuss these problems among yourselves. Then specify in detail the actions which you would propose taking.

CASE 49

Milking Time

The South Victoria Rolling Mills

This Australian firm is a comparatively small, partly-owned and largely autonomous subsidiary of a multi-national concern with headquarters in London. The Australian Chief Executive, George Melhuish, has sent a report to the London board which, when epitomised, reads like this:

"The results this year are disappointing. Profits are down from £91,000 to £14,000 but this does not reflect any adverse change in the market, or our share of it. Labour troubles remain our biggest problem and strikes and disputes continue to take their toll. However, a new and damaging development has arisen over the last 18 months. We have found ourselves hit by a plague of injuries, the bulk of them quite trivial, some even what we can only describe as 'Union inspired'.

"We take the line that, in work like ours, there will always be injuries caused by accidents. In the past, any claims made against the company have been paid by our insurers. Last year, the insurers demanded what we regarded as unreasonable increases — the premiums were raised to £55,000 — more than had been paid out on claims for the two previous years. It seemed logical that we should carry the risk ourselves rather than pay the excessively high premiums. In retrospect that decision was a mistake.

"There was a subsequent mishap in the Belmont foundry which resulted in the loss of three foundrymen's lives and serious injury to two others. Although we offered generous compensation, this was refused as a result of the intervention of the men's Union. This Union is one of the richest — and most militant — in Australia. They were able to afford the most expert and expensive counsel, with the result that we were obliged to pay out what we regard as an extortionate sum (£126,000) in damages. We were advised by our counsel not to appeal against the judgement. This, then, is the main explanation for the deterioration in profits. The problem continues in that our insurers now refuse any sort of cover, nor can we obtain this from any other source. It has become well known in insurance circles that the Union is out to 'milk us dry' in terms of industrial injury compensation.

"One of the finest law firms in Sydney have now offered to act for us. The retaining fee of £15,000 seems excessive, and we are considering all the implications before we make our decision.

"In general we do not feel inclined to be stampeded into any hasty decisions simply as the result of one unfortunate mishap — where the workers were largely responsible for their own misfortune — and a rather punitive Court judgement. We are paying particular attention now to the logging of all accidents — however trivial — including the signing by witnesses wherever possible. All line managers have strict instructions to ensure that safety procedures are carried out."

When the Chief Executive of the Holding Company reads the report he calls a meeting of some of his younger executives. After circulating copies of the report, he says, "I think you'll agree this fellow Melhuish is barking up the wrong tree. I've got to send him a detailed reply to this report. What recommendations do you suggest I make?"

Appreciating that he is currently revising salaries, the executives enter into the spirit of things wholeheartedly.

Questions for the Group to Discuss

1. What would you propose as one of the executives involved in the exercise?
2. Why do you think accidents occur?
3. What is the purpose of recording accidents?
4. What specific information do you think should be recorded when an accident occurs?
5. What role do you think Unions should play in accident prevention?

Main Assignment

Prepare formal notes under appropriate headings such as would be useful if, and when, the Chief Executive asks you for your recommendations.

Subsidiary Assignment

Make a list of the different forms of communication which could be in use between the London company and its Australian subsidiary.

Indicate the relative merits and demerits of each, including costs.

CASE 50

Lies, Damned Lies

Hayford & Mannering plc

Hayford and Mannering are a large engineering firm operating in the West Midlands. When the Managing Director arrives in his office he finds the following items in his in-tray. How do you think he should deal with them?

Written Assignment

After discussing the options prepare a reply to the memorandum received from the Works Manager.

Hayford & Mannering plc
Internal Memorandum

To: Jack Venn Esq.,
    Managing Director

From: Charles Capstan,
Works Manager.
3rd September 1981

Private and Confidential

Last evening as a number of my workpeople were leaving the factory they were presented with a copy of the accompanying leaflet. It is difficult to estimate how many leaflets were distributed. I reckon from what I have heard, about half of the workers leaving the factory were given a copy. Some I know threw them away in disgust. Most seem not to have taken much notice even if they actually read them. But of course the usual bunch of troublemakers are stirring it up for all they are worth.

I have done nothing and said nothing at this stage. I merely send you a copy of the leaflet for your information. If there is any specific action you wish me to take please let me know.

Charles

P.S. The timing of the leaflets is interesting. We start the new round of pay negotiations at the start of next week!

From: Hayford & Mannering
Workers Action Committee

Dear Workmate,

How much did you take home in your pay packet last week? Jack Storringe in the Freezer Division took home £95. Not much left after he's paid for the mortgage and fed and clothed his wife and kids. There's another Jack who works at Hayford & Mannerings. Well, he doesn't actually work. He's the Managing Director. Jack Venn is in a different league. He's one of the bosses and last year he received a salary of £51,750 — plus all the usual directors' perks. Did you know he recently purchased a yacht for £300,000? You and I won't see much of it. It's sailing around the Mediterranean at the moment. That is not the end of the story of course. His family own more shares between them than any other shareholder. And £800,000 was paid out to shareholders in December alone! Poor old Jack Storringe! What a difference a name makes!

When the Union go to Jack Venn with their begging bowl what do you think he is going to say? We can tell you. He always says the same thing. "The company can't afford it!" Isn't it about time we said the same thing to him. "No, Mr Venn, the company can't afford it!"

Did you know that the average wages paid at the Stafford plant are 15% below those at any of six other comparable plants in the West Midlands. There is only one person at Hayford & Mannering who has nothing to complain about. There is no prize for guessing who he is! No doubt Mr. Venn will also say at some point in time, "You are lucky to have a job." We could say the same to him.

CASE 51

The Fairest in the Land

P. J. Felstead & Associates

A London evening newspaper has just published the result of a survey on the general public's attitude to the Trade Unions, and it makes dismal reading for a number of Union leaders who are in town to discuss the formulation of a joint policy towards new legislation in connection with industrial relations which has been proposed. An extract from the survey is given below:

	Percentages		
	Yes	No	Don't know
Do the Unions deliberately make trouble among workpeople?	60	29	11
Should people be obliged to join a Union when they take a job?	27	71	2
Do the Unions do more good than harm?	21	61	18
Do the high wages that Unions get for their members cause unemployment elsewhere?	75	21	4

The Union leaders see the connection between the problem they are dealing with and the findings in the survey. As a result, they decide to approach P. J. Felstead & Associates who are given a brief to discover why the public image of the Unions is so bad. The Senior Partner, Alwyn Griffiths, takes on the assignment himself in the first place, realising that there may be some publicity for the firm emerging. The fee is likely to be quite modest because Alwyn's father was a Labour M.P. in the early post-war years and Alwyn remains a supporter — if slightly less staunch these days. He calls in the workteam for preliminary discussions:

"Look," he says, "I see no point in undertaking any further surveys at this stage. Let's have a Think Tank session. I'll give you 24 hours' notice and we'll spend 2 hours together in this office from 3 o'clock tomorrow afternoon. Don't forget the question. 'Why have the Unions generally got such a bad public image?' And don't forget that we're supposed to be analysts. Let's be objective shall we?''

Assignment

What ideas do you think might emerge from the Think Tank? When you have completed your discussion draft a brief report (say, 5/600 words) such as might rank as a contribution to the final report.

CASE 52

Heads and Tails

Grimsdyke Alloys Ltd.

Frank Pavitt is the Minister of State with special responsibility for improving the climate of industrial relations. He is very concerned to do everything possible to reduce the amount of unrest in industry. He realises the problem goes far deeper than strikes and so-called "industrial action". He wants to reduce absenteeism, shoddy workmanship, negative attitudes and anything else which reduces the level of industrial production. For this purpose, he invites a number of industrialists to a formal dinner in the hope and expectation that between them they will be able to produce some useful ideas.

One of the industrialists invited to the dinner is Sir George Trevithick, Chairman and Managing Director of Grimsdyke Alloys, one of the largest engineering groups in the country. He has called a special Board Meeting and you represent the Directors attending this meeting. Sir George tells you about the invitation he has received:

> "The new Minister has made a special point that any advice we offer should be related to the industry as a whole," he explains, "though obviously we shall give advice based on our own experience. This seems an excellent opportunity to make our views known in high places, gentlemen, and I thought you would welcome the chance to discuss things with me before I dine with Mr. Pavitt and his colleagues tomorrow. I shall have Grimsdyke's interests in mind at all times I can assure you, but on this occasion I shall be expected to make suggestions as to what the Government might do to help improve the general climate of industrial relations in the country at large."

Your Chairman now asks you to contribute your ideas.

Assignment

When you have finished the discussion complete a Report Form setting out the options and their relative merits and demerits.

157

Compendium

Absenteeism (rate of)

In order to measure the extent of absenteeism, many firms calculate their rate of absenteeism. The calculation is made thus:

$$\frac{\text{Number of days lost through job absence during the period}}{\text{Average number of employees} \times \text{number of workdays during the period}} \times 100$$

The percentage arrived at can then be compared to previous periods and/or absentee rates in other departments/firms.

The Board of Directors

This is the Company's chief policy-making body. The directors are individually elected to the Board by the shareholders at a General Meeting. The Board fixes the objectives for the Company and appoints the senior executives including the Managing Director. The Board will function as a committee in reaching its decisions. Formal resolutions will be passed and each director will have one vote, regardless of his/her shareholdings.

A non-executive director is one who does not have departmental responsibilities, and may serve on a number of different boards.

Bullock Report 1977 (Cmnd 6706)

This was the Report of the Committee of Inquiry on Industrial Democracy, commonly known as the Bullock Report after its chairman, Lord Bullock. The majority of the members of the committee recommended the introduction of legislation to give employees a right to be represented on the boards of management of companies with 2000 or more employees. There was a lukewarm reception for the proposals on both sides of industry.

Decentralisation

A technique whereby there is a maximum delegation of authority and a minimum control over what is delegated. In a large-scale business there must be some control exercised by the central/higher authority, but with decentralisation, such control is kept to a minimum. An example of decentralisation is where a global sum is allocated for annual expenditure, leaving the local units to spend at their own discretion. Note that decentralisation relates to decision-making powers — not to geographic dispersion.

Merits of decentralisation:

1. It develops self-reliance and initiative on the part of the junior managers. It can be seen as a form of management training.
2. Decisions are made close to the scene of action.
3. Leadership of the operational unit is made easier when workers see that the operational unit manager has the power to make worth-while decisions.

However, in any large organisation, certain controls will have to be imposed in order to co-ordinate divergent activities and to maintain the uniformity and quality of decisions. Devices which centralise power include:

(a) standardised procedures   (b) instruction manuals
(c) budgetary controls   (d) random inspections
(e) recording and reporting of decisions made.

Differentials

It is not only absolute wages which are of interest to workers. They are also greatly aware of what other workers are being paid. Thus, if a skilled worker in a particular factory is offered an extra £10 a week — the same amount as unskilled workers — he is likely to be aggrieved. From the following statistics it can be seen that he would require an increase of £15 a week in order to retain his existing advantage — or differential:

	Present weekly wage (£)	Proposed increase (£)	Increase required to retain differential (£)
Skilled grade	150	10	15
Unskilled grade	100	10	10

Discipline

In order to achieve the results expected of him and by which he will be judged, a manager or supervisor needs to give instructions which are obeyed. Ideally these instructions will be obeyed willingly but where there is resistance or reluctance, the manager or supervisor should be able to apply suitable sanctions (punishments).
In the words of Robert C. Appleby:*

*Modern Business Administration, *Pitman Publishing*, Second Edition, 1976.

"Disciplinary action should contribute towards improved behaviour, but certain matters must be noted:
  (a) Behaviour expected must be *made known* and this is best done in the period of induction.
  (b) Discipline should be exercised *fairly*, with no favouritism or excessive penalties, and as *soon after* the breach as possible. (Some methods of disciplining are by reprimand, downgrading, suspension, refusing a wage increase, transfer or dismissal.)
  (c) Management should not break rules itself. A good example is essential.
  (d) The quality of discipline can vary with the type of leadership and the understanding of the common purpose of the organisation."

Discrimination

Since the *Sex Discrimination Act 1975* became law every contract of employment is deemed to include an "equality clause". The result is that whenever a woman is employed on "like work" or "work rated as equivalent" with that of a man in the same employment she is entitled to the same rate of pay. But the Act also applies to such things as overtime pay, bonuses, shift work allowances, luncheon vouchers, sick pay schemes and other fringe benefits, as well as hours of work, holidays and terms of notice.

The onus of establishing "like work" is on the applicant, and it is always open to an employer to refute the claim on the grounds that a male worker is being paid more for "heavy" work, or that the extra payments are to reward higher skills or qualifications or long service.

An employee who feels she is not receiving equal treatment under the Act and is unable to settle the matter amicably with her employer can take her case to an Industrial Tribunal. One such case is recorded as Brodie v. Startrite Engineering Co. Ltd. (1976). There were two women employed as drill operators by the Startrite Engineering Co. They were paid 71.3p per hour and went to an Industrial Tribunal to claim parity with a male worker who was paid just over £1 per hour. The employer's contention was that the different rate was justified because the male worker had the ability to obtain the appropriate jig and drill to set his own machine and that he was also able to sharpen and replace drills. Furthermore, he was able to carry out minor repairs which relieved his charge-hand of some responsibilities. The Tribunal rejected the womens' applications and accepted the argument of the employer that the difference in pay was "genuinely due to a material difference other than the difference of sex".

The Race Relations Act 1976 is aimed at discouraging discrimination against people on the grounds of their race or ethnic origins.

Both acts will need to be borne in mind in regard to:

(a) advertisements for staff;
(b) recruitment and selection of staff;
(c) training and opportunities for promotion;
(d) determining rates of pay.

Dismissal

Employees must receive a written statement setting out the terms and conditions of their employment. The statement will include a job title which could become relevant if the employee is subsequently dismissed for refusing to do something different. This statement becomes the basis for the contract between employer and employee. But the legislation accords the employee certain rights. For example, any employee who is dismissed may be entitled to compensation where the dismissal is wrongful, unfair or the result of redundancy.

(a) Wrongful dismissal

There is a right to claim damages for a breach of contract whenever a contract has been terminated without proper notice. The appropriate notice may be specified in the contract mentioned above, but the Contracts of Employment Act 1972 sets out minimum periods of notice, viz.:

(i) For those who have been employed by the organisation between *four weeks* and *two years*: one week's notice.
(ii) For others: *one week's notice for every year of employment* (with a maximum of twelve weeks).

The right to pursue a claim for wrongful dismissal is a common law right and is dealt with in the civil courts. Industrial Tribunals have no jurisdiction.

(b) Unfair dismissal

There is an implied term in every contract of employment that the employee will obey his employer's lawful commands and give honest and faithful service. Failure to do so will justify dismissal. But under the *Trade Union and Labour Relations Act 1974*, it is for the employer to prove that the dismissal was fair. If he cannot do so, then the dismissal must be unfair. In general, dismissal will be accepted as fair so long as the employer can prove the employee's misconduct or inadequacy, or where there is necessary redundancy.

Where an employee claims there has been an unfair dismissal, the case will be considered by an Industrial Tribunal (composed of a legally-qualified chairman and two laymen representing each side of industry). In order to prove fair dismissal, an employer would need to show, firstly that he had a fair reason for dismissing the employee and, secondly that he dealt with the problem in a reasonable way. Thus, where there has been misconduct, the employee will have to have been given the opportunity for an explanation, unless there are disciplinary procedures within the organisation which have been followed. Similarly, where an employee has been dismissed for inefficiency there would need to have been appropriate warnings. The warnings do not have to be in writing but written warnings provide better evidence.

Remedies for unfair dismissal are:

Reinstatement, which puts the claimaint back into a position as if there had been no dismissal.

Re-engagement, which becomes necessary when reinstatement is not an available option. The nature of the work offered will be as close as possible to the previous job.

Compensation, which is in part based on age, salary and length of service (the basic award) and in part on the extent of the financial loss suffered by the claimant (the compensatory award).

Employment Tests

In many selection procedures, tests have been devised to assess attributes such as intelligence or aptitude for particular tasks. The aptitudes to be tested will be directly related to the job to be done but might include one or more of the following:

(i) manual dexterity;
(ii) appropriate clerical skills;
(iii) general reasoning ability;
(iv) social and oral skills.

Manual dexterity tests are used to test applicants for work involving assembly, packing and repetitive machine operations. Whenever candidates will be expected to operate particular equipment such as word processors or telephone switchboards, some practical demonstration of skills would be valuable, though the problem is to avoid disrupting workflows.

General reasoning tests are sometimes used to test the applicants' ability to resolve problems. On the one hand are the Eysenck-type tests designed to provide an I.Q. rating. On the other hand are situational tests. These simulate key aspects of a job and might, for example, take the form of an "in-basket" exercise where each person taking the test is asked to deal with a typical battery of memoranda, letters and reports. They would be asked to respond with appropriate replies, having been given adequate background data.

Social and oral skills can be tested in a group situation:*

> ". . . A group of candidates for a job (usually of a supervisory or executive type) are placed in a room, given a practical problem to discuss and solve, and observed by others. The observers note how they interact with one another. Who had the most useful ideas? Who emerged as a leader? Who conciliated opposing views? Who was most convincing in oral expression? These and many other qualities are noted by the observers. The group oral performance test makes it possible to evaluate effectiveness and skill in interpersonal relations."

Ergonomics

This is the study of man in relation to his work. It involves the fitting together of men and equipment. It brings together two groups of specialists — those who know about human capacities and weaknesses and those who design equipment. Apart from the design of machines, Ergonomics is concerned with general working conditions such as lighting, noise and temperature. These are important factors not only for ensuring the health and safety of the operators but also for efficient operation. The aim is to make man and machine an efficient production unit. The ergonomist contributes by:

(i) designing the prototype and
(ii) modifying existing equipment.

Flexible Working Hours

Each employee is able to choose, within prescribed limits, the starting and finishing times of work each day. Employees must attend during the coretime each day, but the remaining hours can be absorbed within the flexbands — as they feel inclined (Fig 13).

---

*Dale S. Beach, *Personnel — The Management of People at Work* Collier Macmillan, London, Second Edition, 1970.

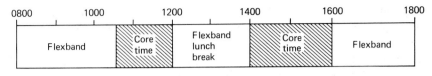

FIG 13

For example, Sally may start work late — at 0930 — take an hour for lunch (1300–1400) and leave work at 1800. This would give her a standard 37½ hour working week. By contrast, Julie might prefer to start early — at 0800 — taking half an hour for lunch (1200–1230) and breaking off at 1600.

It is useful device for those with commuting problems and domestic responsibilities.

The Health and Safety at Work Act 1974

The duty of employers to safeguard their workers is rooted in common law, but following the Thalidomide tragedy (1963), the Aberfan disaster (1966), and the Flixborough explosion (1974) Parliament decided to introduce legislation to ensure that the highest standards of safety were applied to work situations. The main effect of the act is fourfold:

1. To extend the employer's duty to encompass the health and welfare of people who come into contact with the enterprise.
2. To place an onus on the employee to take resonable care of the health and safety of himself and others.
3. To bring in the possibility of criminal prosecution (an unlimited fine and/or two years' prison sentence) where there is a breach of duty.
4. To set up a system whereby existing legislation is progressively replaced by a series of regulations and approved codes of practice.

However, the principle legislation affecting offices remains at this stage *The Offices, Shops and Railway Premises Act 1963*. Among its provisions are:

S.5   "No room shall be overcrowded. . . . The number of persons shall not be such that the quotient derived by dividing by that number the number which expresses in square feet the area of the surface of the floor . . . is less than forty or the quotient derived by dividing by the first-mentioned number the number which expresses in cubic feet the capacity of the room is less than four hundred." In other words each person in an office must have $11.5m^3$ of space and $3.75m^2$ of floor area.

S.6   "A temperature of less than 16° Centigrade shall not be deemed, after the first hour, to be a reasonable temperature while work is going on."

There shall be. . . .

S.7   "Adequate supplies of fresh or artificially purified air. . . ."

S.8   "Suitable lighting, whether natural or artificial . . . glazed windows and skylights shall be kept clean. . . . and free from obstruction . . ."

S.9   "Suitable and sufficient sanitary conveniences . . . at places conveniently accessible. . . . clean and properly maintained. . . ."

S.10/13 "Accessible washing facilities. . . . running hot and cold water, soap and clean towels. . . ."
        "Means of escape. . . . conspicuously marked. . . . appropriate means of fighting fire placed as to be readily available . . ."

S.48   "Notice. . . . sent to the appropriate (local) authority . . . where an accident causes loss of life or . . . disables any person for more than three days from doing normal work . . ."

Holding Company

A company may own shares in another company and may acquire sufficient of the voting shares to be able to elect the other Company's Board of Directors. In this case, it becomes known as a holding company. The company which is controlled is described as a subsidiary. The subsidiary may itself control another Company or Companies, the latter becoming sub-subsidiaries. The total organisation — holding company and subsidiaries becomes known as a Group.

Interviewing

The interview situation should have three clear objectives:

(1) To give the applicant an opportunity to find out more about the job and the organisation.
(2) To compare the candidates with the job/person specification to find out how closely they match.
(3) To compare the candidates with each other so that the most suitable applicant(s) can be chosen.

The candidates are only able to judge the people they are being invited to work with by the contacts they make during the selection procedures. P. W. Betts indicates some of the ways in which a friendly yet business-like atmosphere can be encouraged:*

> "The interview room should be designed to put the candidate at ease: comfortable, no glare from lighting, and an avoidance of 'inquisition' settings. Similarly, the waiting room should be comfortable, with access to cloakrooms, refreshments if required, and reading material. . . . A quick exchange of information on a familiar topic relieves the tension a little. . . . Speak clearly . . . Give the applicant time to think. . . . Listen. . . . Concentrate. . . . Avoid digressing . . . lengthy speeches . . . personal views."

Job Description — see Recruitment and Selection

Job Rotation

Instead of keeping each worker on the same task day after day, they are interchanged to give them some variety in their work. For example, Matthew, Mark and John may be required to perform tasks A, B and C continuously. The jobs may be rotated as follows:

Day	1	2	3	4	5
Matthew	A	A	B	B	C
Mark	B	B	C	C	A
John	C	C	A	A	B

The merits of job rotation are that:

(a) It facilitates the cover of jobs at holiday times and when there is sickness.
(b) It might increase productivity where the jobs are boring and easy to learn.
(c) It gives the manager greater flexibility in the use of his staff.
(d) It can be used in a development programme — for managers as well as workers.

Job Specification — see Recruitment and Selection

Labour Turnover (rate of)

When employees leave an organisation, expense is incurred in recruiting

*From *Staff Management*, Macdonald & Evans, 1977.

replacements. For this reason, many of the larger firms monitor the numbers voluntarily leaving the organisation. The calculation is made as follows:

$$\frac{\text{Number of employees leaving during the period}}{\text{Average number of employees}} \times 100$$

This figure can then be compared over a period of time — and with other departments/firms.

Line Managers/Supervisors

These are the staff in charge of the operational units. They are the shop floor managers. They control the assembly lines in the factory or manage the branches of retail stores. They can be contrasted with the so-called staff officers who are the specialists offering advice from headquarters. There is sometimes a conflict between the line managers who are at the scene of the action — and tend to be all-rounders — and the experts who propose but are not required to implement their proposals.

Management by Objectives

If we accept that decentralisation brings life to a business, we need to find a way of delegating authority without losing essential control. Many progressive organisations turn to selective target setting as the solution. The germ of the idea is contained in budgetary control with its concept of financial accountability and cost centres. Management retains control of the area with which it is mainly concerned, namely results. Standards of performance are determined for each Division, department and/or section of the organisation. Thus, the Metal Products Division in an engineering group may be given a target of £x million profit. This will be broken down into constituent slices of revenues and costs for every section of the Division until each individual executive knows what he/she is expected to achieve. An integrated plan is developed for the whole organisation.

Management by Objectives has the following features:

1. A list of written requirements for action is drawn up in conjunction with the subordinate manager.
2. A subsequent formal discussion between the superior and subordinate takes place to consider how far the written requirements have been met.

3. The subordinate starts the period in question knowing exactly what is expected of him/her, and ultimately knows what is expected of his/her performance.
4. The parties to the discussion are encouraged to look ahead and try to anticipate problems rather than wait for them to happen.
5. Responsibilities are committed to paper. In other words, delegation is clearly defined.
6. Targets can be pinpointed so that efforts are concentrated on those areas which senior managers see as vital. These might concentrate on profits in the higher echelons — or levels of wastage, reduction in absenteeism or labour turnover at operational levels.
7. Schedules can be revised if and when the situations change during the period of the plan.

Manpower Planning

This is the overall plan for staffing and is normally built into a system of budgetary control. A full system of budgetary control entails comprehensive forecasts including sales targets and matching production schedules. Tied in with these long-term plans are the financial implications of the programme and the manpower needs required to fulfill it. Cost centres are developed and the financial constraints provide the parameter for the staffing plan for the various departments in the organisation. C. J. Coulson-Thomas emphasizes the need for economic use of human resources:*

> "An increase in the number of employees leads to increased expenditure upon remuneration, fringe benefits, accommodation, supervision and training, travelling, consumable stores, organisation and administration. Many categories of expense vary more or less directly with the number of employees. Manpower planning involves looking carefully at the implications of management decisions for manning levels and the possibilities of achieving a more efficient utilisation of manpower."

When comparatively small numbers of staff are involved, responsibility for the Personnel function might be assumed by the Senior Executive or by one of the Personal Assistants. In either case the person(s) concerned would find themselves undertaking many or all of the tasks we have been considering here.

*From Company Administration Made Simple, W. H. Allen, 1975.

Music at Work

Ideas?

(a) Plot output over the course of a typical day to discover when music could be uplifting. Consider, for example, the following plot of output (Fig. 14). When would you suggest music be played?

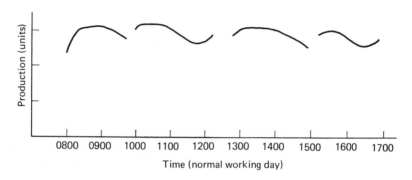

FIG 14

(b) Ask workers what they would prefer — through Works Council, shop stewards etc. Do you think their choices would conflict with (a)?

(c) Why not have a factory disc jockey (unpaid) — or a linked programme with other members in the Group — messages on weddings, birthdays etc? But would noise level allow this sort of programme?

(d) Introduce the new programme on a trial basis — keep a log of "comments" received from the workers or their representatives.

(e) Invite workers to supply their own tapes and records.

(f) Have a "Top Twenty" for the factory with the workers voting for them.

(g) Monitor the effect of the programme on production levels to make sure it is having the desired effect.

Natural wastage

One way in which the number of workers can be reduced without making any redundant is to let staff leave without attempting to replace them. Thus, if 20% of the staff leave during the course of a normal year, within two and a half years the workforce would be halved.

Nepotism

Many businesses start off as one man enterprises. An individual provides the capital and enterprise initially and being the founder it is understandable if members of the family receive preference when jobs are allocated. The use of the term nepotism, however, indicates that undue favour is given in such appointments.

Recruitment and Selection

A position becomes available as a result of:

(a) the exit of an existing member of staff through leaving the organisation, transfer within the organisation or retirement.
(b) the creation of a new post or posts as a result of expansion.

The first stage in the employment process is to prepare a *job description* which includes the job title, the section or department in which it is found and its position in the hierarchy. The main tasks are described and for this purpose, consultation with the line supervisor/manager will be required. The content will depend on the purpose of the description, bearing in mind that it could be used for planning and evaluation as well as recruitment. Apart from the description of mechanical tasks such as "filing" or "interviewing clients" the description should refer to any special equipment to be used and any special qualities required. The job description is normally used to prepare any advertisements for the post.

A *job (or person) specification* will be drawn up for the interviewer and although this will be based on the job description, it will concentrate on the personal attributes and qualifications sought in any applicant. One expects to find matters such as physical appearance, work experience, general intelligence, temperament and application included in the framework for analysis.

Redundancy

Employees who have been made redundant are entitled to compensation providing that:

(i) The employer has ceased to carry on business altogether or at the place where the employee has contracted to work, or,
(ii) the need for the particular kind of work has ceased, or diminished, or is expected to do so.

Payment is according to the following scale, assuming a minimum of *two years* continuous employment and a maximum reckonable service of *twenty years*:

½ a week's pay for each complete year worked between
the ages of 18 and 21
1 week's pay for each complete year worked between
the ages of 22 and 40
1½ week's pay for each complete year worked between
the ages of 41 and 59 (women)
and 41 and 64 (men).

The detailed rights and obligations of the parties are set out in the *Redundancy Payments Act 1965*.

References

These are usually taken up before the interviews so that the selector(s) can relate them to the physically present candidates. However, it would be unwise to place too much store by the comments because:
  (a) Referees are no doubt aware of the legal complications if they put any adverse comments in writing (they could find themselves sued for defamation of character *inter alia*).
  (b) It is difficult to interpret comments from strangers meaningfully. Some referees will be lavish with their praises. Others will give credit grudgingly. To what extent are you expected to read between the lines?
  (c) It has been known for first-class staff to be given bad references by employers who do not wish to lose them and, conversely, some employers have been known to give glowing references for staff they are glad to lose.

Remuneration

While pay is only one of the factors affecting motivation in the work-place, it is a very sensitive area. Staff are not only concerned with the pay they receive. They are just as concerned with differentials (i.e. how their pay compares with other peoples'). Fair treatment is expected though there are obvious difficulties in trying to achieve this. Most organisations offer a system of structured salaries based on some form of job grading. Key jobs are analysed and a technique known as *job evaluation* is applied. For example, a particular job might be given a points rating such as 12 for the degree of responsibility involved, 10 points for the special training required, 6 points for a rather unfavourable working environment. The total scored is then compared with the ratings for other jobs, and related equitably to an appropriate salary scale.

The Institute of Administrative Management proposes an alternative system for offices using six different grades for the various jobs:

A Grade — Tasks requiring no previous clerical experience — closely directed.

B Grade — Tasks carried out in accordance with a limited number of well-defined rules after a few weeks' training.

C Grade — Tasks requiring a reasonable degree of experience or a special aptitude.

D Grade — Tasks calling for considerable experience and a limited degree of initiative but carried out according to a pre-determined procedure.

E Grade — Tasks requiring a significant measure of discretion and initiative, specialised knowledge and individual responsibility.

F Grade — Tasks carrying extensive responsibility and judgement and requiring professional skills (legal, accounting etc.)

This can be accompanied by a system of *merit rating* so that there is within each of the main grades a sub-classification:

Beginners rank as Grade 1
Qualified rank as Grade 2
Experienced rank as Grade 3
Superior rank as Grade 4
Those ready for promotion rank as Grade 5

Shop stewards

The shop steward is elected by a show of hands from his fellow trade unionists in a particular workshop. His functions are:

(i) To inspect union cards and see that contributions are up to date.
(ii) To act as a recruiting officer.
(iii) To ensure that agreements between management and union are enforced.
(iv) To represent fellow workers who have grievances.

The value of shop stewards to management:

(a) Management may learn of grievances quickly — and take remedial action promptly. Dealings with external unions are likely to be slow in comparison.

(b) Small problems are less likely to become big ones?

But they also create problems:

(a) Who is in charge? Is it the foremen/supervisor — or the shop steward?

(b) Unlike the national officers of the union they cannot see the global/overall picture — they may play into the hands of the employers.

Staff Appraisal

The prime purpose of staff appraisal should always be to improve performance — both individually and collectively. A manager will need to evaluate performance in order to determine the sort of action required to improve the future effectiveness of staff. There is always likely to be a gap between what is achieved and what could be achieved and the manager is required to minimise this shortfall. It has to be borne in mind that the business organisation is normally hierarchical and that the manager's performance — achieved through his subordinates — is also subject to surveillance.

Formal appraisal is often linked with a periodic wage or salary review. Where there is a pay scale with some sort of efficiency bar the question might be simply, "Has the member of staff worked well enough to be given the further increment?" Or where there is a grading system the question might be, "Is this person ready to be upgraded?" In these instances the purpose of the appraisal is to decide between a yes or a no response.

Appraisal might also be required in connection with promotion or transfer with a view to determining the suitability of the candidate.

Various factors such as workrate, accuracy, attendance and co-operativeness will need to be brought into account in the appraisal, but it is difficult to decide the weighting for each of these. There should be a high degree of uniformity in the application of these factors if they are to be seen and accepted as fair. Some staff might even accept criticism more easily if the appraisal is by an impartial "outsider".

One of the major problems facing the manager is to link the appraisal process with appropriate guidance for the staff so that they are fully informed as to:

(i) The extent to which their performance has been satisfactory.

(ii) What is precisely expected from them in the future.

(iii) How future targets can be achieved.

Staff who are disappointed at the outcome of the appraisal may leave the organisation or lower the standard of their work. For poor staff to leave is a favourable outcome, but on no account can it said to be a successful operation when continuing staff lose motivation. The problem for the manager is to ensure that the appraisal system stimulates and encourages rather than having the opposite effect.

Another problem in assessing staff is to find meaningful standards by which performances can be assessed. The standards must be identifiable, understood and measurable. While some work is easily measured, there is a great deal of administration which is difficult to gauge in quantifiable terms. And where there is group work, individual contributions may prove difficult to evaluate. The danger is that appraisal can become subjective and personal rather than objective and dispassionate.

Staff Development

The physical assets of the business are inanimate. By contrast, human beings are highly sensitive and will respond to praise or criticism. Since one of the prime functions of management is to motivate staff, a programme of counselling and training will be called for. If staff are given the right sort of encouragement the following benefits can be expected to accrue:

   (i) The performance of staff will improve when staff are able to accept more responsibility. The application of F. Herzberg's Hygiene-motivation Concept at Bell Telephone, Texas Instruments, and I.C.I. has substantiated this notion.

  (ii) When senior positions become vacant there will be internal candidates available who are already familiar with work patterns and procedures. This will be a particularly favourable situation in the event of serious illness or unexpected departure.

(iii) Staff will need to adapt to changing work patterns and procedures. This calls for a willingness to learn which is not likely to prevail unless the staff see opportunities for self-improvement.

 (iv) Where the M.B.O. technique is employed staff development is part of the system.

Staff Records

Individual records will be required for staff for the following reasons:

 (a) To give Managers/Supervisors a reminder of the history, qualifications, performance, training and interests of staff.

 (b) To note important financial data such as rates of pay, wages/salary paid, tax code (indicating tax deductions to be made from pay), accumulated pay and tax suffered for the year to date (the tax year ends on the 5th April), deductions for occupational pension funds, and voluntary deductions for savings schemes etc.

(c) To provide data for Managers/Supervisors dealing with disciplinary matters, promotions or references for staff who are leaving or have left.

Staff records in the larger firm are likely to be computerised but additionally or alternatively there might be a visible card index system or a folder for each member of staff. Where confidential information is included such as reports and appraisals, family background etc. the records will need to be adequately secured.

Trade Unions

A trade union is an organisation which consists of workers whose main purpose is to regulate the relations between the workers and their employers. Most unions have a national executive council or committee elected by, or responsible to the annual conference of delegates from local branches. Below the national level there are usually regional, district or area organisations, while at the level of the individual member, the local branch functions. The TUC (Trade Union Congress) is in effect, a confederation of unions.

"Unions often provide dispute benefit (strike pay) for members involved in official industrial action. They also provide legal advice for members who suffer injury or contract diseases at work, and may pay members' legal costs when a case for compensation goes to court. Some unions pay benefits in case of illness, accident, death and retirement (additional to those payable under the Government's national insurance scheme), financed out of membership contributions. . . . Trade unions may devote funds to political objects subject to certain conditions. These funds are primarily used to support candidates in local or national elections."*

Training

When staff join the organisation their talents and skills will not be fully utilised until they have adapted to their new environment. They will need

Industrial Relations, Central office of Information, HMSO, 1977.

to be familiarised with their surroundings, their workmates, their equipment and what for them are strange work procedures. This should be the purpose of an *induction programme* and it will be advisable to allocate an experienced member of staff to "nurse" the newcomer through the difficult early days.

However, a continuous programme of training might be envisaged for all members of staff on the following grounds:

1. Expertise will need to be updated as new technologies and workflows are introduced. The Personnel Department will normally be responsible for organising courses either on-job (within the organisation) or off-job (at technical colleges etc.).
2. By exchanging jobs, tedium can be reduced at the same time that new skills are acquired.
3. Job rotation will allow a greater staff mobility and provide cover for staff who are absent; planned (holidays etc.) or unplanned (sickness etc.).
4. Every opportunity should be taken to improve the performance of staff in their existing tasks.

The Industrial Training Act of 1964 set up machinery for the establishment of *Industrial Training Boards* for industry and commerce to provide training courses and other facilities for employees in their respective industries. The ITBs pay grants to employers providing training of an approved standard, the funds being raised by a levy on all employers in the industry. The Employment and Training Act 1973 created the Manpower Services Commission, made up of representatives from both sides of industry and from the educational system. The Commission has taken over responsibility for employment and training throughout industry and commerce. The 1973 Act also exempted from the levy smaller firms and those with adequate training programmes of their own. Levies are now limited to 1 per cent of the payroll unless Parliament agrees to a higher rate.

Welfare

A concern for the well-being of staff is both civilised and rewarding from the employer's point of view. Included in the area of welfare we would expect to find the following services:

(i) *Counselling* — most employees will find themselves facing personal problems at some time or other and both employer and employee will benefit if the problem can be talked over. An anxious employee is unlikely to be an efficient worker. The role of the counsellor can be compared to that of the psychiatrist in that both will be expected to listen sympathetically. However, the wise counsellor will avoid offering advice other than to suggest that the "patient" refers to an appropriate expert.

(ii) *Recreational facilities* — including sports facilities, library facilities and rest rooms. Breaks can be very beneficial in terms of staff performance and managements should ensure that a favourable environment is provided.

(iii) *Medical services* — these are sometimes provided in the larger organisations. The aim is to reduce absenteeism and lateness.

(iv) *Physical welfare* — dealing with the provision of canteen and washroom facilities, créches for young children, etc.

Guidelines

The frameworks given below are intended as aids to discussion — if aids are needed. They should be seen as indicators of the approach which might be adopted and the points which might be made rather than prescribed solutions. They might similarly serve as bases for the written reports where these are required.

Of course, tutors may well wish to vary the approach. They may provide from their own knowledge of the students' background a framework which will be more appropriate to the training needs of the group tackling the exercise.

CASE 1

1.C, 2.A, 3.D. 4.B

CASE 2

Cameo One

Appropriate responses (depending on the store's policy) would include:

1. "I'm sorry to hear that, Madam. What sort of doll was it? Can you fetch it back to the store at some time? We'll have a look at it. We might be able to send it back to the manufacturer. . . . If you can bring the receipt with you . . . Could I have your name please? . . ."

   Follow up — Give details to Buyer/Manager of Toy Department.

2. "I'm very sorry to hear that, sir. If you give me your name and telephone number. I'll get in touch with our Television Department immediately and make sure that someone responsible gets back to you as soon as possible. Will you give me ten minutes, or a quarter of an hour to make enquiries. . . ."

   Follow up — Contact Manager/Deputy of TV Department immediately. Check to find out that action has been taken.

3. "I expect the letters crossed. Can I have your name and address. . . . and your 'phone number please? If we don't ring you back you'll know the cheque arrived safely.

   Follow up — Check with Accounts Department immediately.

4. "It's so difficult in these cases, Madam. Once you've left the counter it's almost impossible to check. . . . but our young lady shouldn't have been rude. Can you give me as much detail as you can? And your name and telephone number please?

Follow up — Report details to Manager of Hosiery Department.

5. "Can I have your name please?. . . . and your 'phone number? Well sir/madam I don't know anything about the advertisement but I will ask the Manager of our Carpet Department to ring you back.

Follow up — Ask Carpet Manager to telephone the customer. Check diplomatically that he/she has done so.

An Alternative Treatment

Of course it could be argued that it would be better for complaints to go directly to the department in question, as would normal enquiries. A list of pros and cons could be drawn up to compare the alternatives.

Cameo Two (a few further examples)

Telephone	Speed	No record of communication
	Questions can be asked (feedback)	Lack of time for consideration
	Cheaper at certain times and if call is brief	
Letter	Comparatively cheap	Delivery takes days (weeks for overseas mail)
	Copies can be filed	Responses slow

CASE 3

Trip to the States

Options available to Tony Philips are to send:

			Pros (for)		*Cons (against)*
(a)	Colin Grant	(i)	personable	(i)	lack of qualifications?
		(ii)	useful connections	(ii)	a womaniser?
(b)	Peter Crisp	(i)	Keen to go?	(i)	stable background?
		(ii)	well qualified?	(ii)	misunderstands family's role
(c)	John Lampard	(i)	would give him self respect?	(i)	alcoholic?
		(ii)	removes an obstacle?	(ii)	unwilling?

				(iii)	his expertise is needed here?
(d)	Himself	(i)	No. 1 priority?	(i)	an absent leader?
		(ii)	should show willing?	(ii)	danger of a 'takeover' in his absence?

Recommendations

Tony should interview his subordinates before reaching a conclusion — but in which order should he see them?
He should also consult the Sales Director. Why? Should he consult him before or after he has interviewed the subordinates?

CASE 4

Women at Work: Case Study

No obvious choice, but when Head Office have made their decision the unsuccessful candidate might be interviewed and future prospects discussed.

CASE 5

Promotion and Gladys Benson

Options for David Riggs:

A^1 Talk to Gladys *now*. How is her mother? There is a human tragedy here. How is this situation likely to affect her work? She may stop work if her mother dies. Put her "in the picture"?

A^2 Ask her to apply for the job? Confirm that she has your backing? The loyalty of other staff is at risk.

B^1 Wait until the advertisement appears before taking any action?

B^2 Ask Head Office for an explanation of the "50% rule"?

B^3 Approach Head Office for clarification of Gladys Benson's position?

B^4 Put the case for Gladys' promotion to Head Office?

B^5 Wait and see the sort of candidates who are short-listed for the post? The *best* person for the job should be appointed?

Note: It is unlawful for an employer to discriminate on grounds of sex (Sex Discrimination Act, 1975).

CASE 6

Bawls and Smalls

Figure 15 should held to explain the main merit of the créche for the young mother who is obliged to go to work:

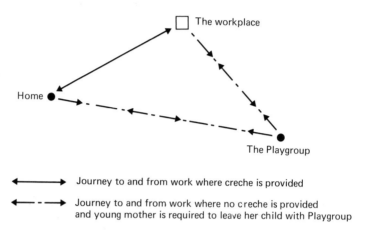

FIG 15

An evaluation of the créche system could include the following points:

Pros	Cons
1. Less absenteeism and labour turnover.	1. Professional childminders would be required.
2. Improved workrate.	2. Workplace space is required.
3. Beneficiaries could be charged to defray cost.	3. Mothers would require access to their children during workhours.
4. An aid to recruitment.	4. What about the staff without babies?

CASE 7

Hornet's Nest

Options available to John Cowdrey were:

		Pros	*Cons*
(a)	to support supervisor	would help her to establish discipline	would encourage "scapegoating"
(b)	to support April Anderson	would help to establish a relaxed atmosphere among younger staff	would undermine supervisor's authority
(c)	to attempt a judgment	justice would be done	difficulty in separating fact and fiction
(d)	to leave supervisor to solve the problem herself	would encourage an independent attitude	would make supervisor feel she could not depend on her manager's support in a crisis

Recommendations

If John wants to improve the atmosphere, his subordinates would need to know what he expected from them. He would presumably be expected to support them in a crisis? Has his supervisor had time to settle in? But there is a long-term problem here. John should discuss with his supervisor plans for monitoring future output and behaviour of staff.

CASE 8

Star Performance

Options available to Jane Garner

Problem 1

A. Inform Head Office.
B. Consult Alberto:
   (i) to find out the facts.
   (ii) and offer more pay.
   (iii) and offer job to daughter.
   (iv) and offer accommodation for daughter.
C. Delay Alberto's departure:
   (i) in the hope of reconciliation.
   (ii) pointing out that daughter will need financial support.
   (iii) advising him to keep his options open.
   (iv) letting him know how vital he is to the hotel.
D. Do nothing until Manager's return.

Problem 2

   A. Inform Head Office.
   B. Wait for Manager's return.
   C. Carry out investigation and if fraud is discovered:
      (i) report findings to Head Office.
      (ii) report findings to manager on his return.

Problem 3

   A. Ask honeymooners to switch rooms with compensation in the form
      of:
      (i) cash reduction.
      (ii) some free (or special) meals etc.
   B. Ask disappointed guest to accept alternative accommodation with:
        (i) significant cash reduction.
        (ii) "royal treatment".
   C. This is likely to be a fairly common situation? What usually happens
      when there is a double booking?

Problem 4

   A. Consult staff.
   B. Inform the police.
   C. Compensate guests.
   D. Post warnings (what is the law on this subject?)
   E. Publicise the fact that watch is being kept.

Problem 5

Have a quiet word with the waitress in question explaining the importance of maintaining the hotel's reputation for courtesy — even under pressure.

CASE 9

Materialism: Case Study

Evaluation from company's point of view:

For	*Against*
1. If supplemental could give additional motivation.	1. Distinctions between "easy" and "difficult" rounds would make scheme inequitable.
2. The company wins either way — prizes only if sales increase.	2. Would need to ensure that programme was cost-effective
3. Would reduce labour turnover.	3. If goods offered take too much effort the roundsmen will lose interest.
4. Ego food for roundsmen.	
5. Family pressures on roundsmen?	4. If goods on offer are too mundane they will not inspire the roundsmen.
6. Recognition for achievement.	
7. Fosters a competitive spirit.	5. Sales could be forced at the expense of customer goodwill.
8. Goods would be at a favourable discount.	7. Non-sales staff are excluded.
9. The firm promoting the scheme would need to justify the scheme.	8. If roundsmen received cash they could buy what they wanted.

Implementation?

(a) Prior consultation with roundsmen's representatives.
(b) Clarify tax position — would the prizes count as earnings?
(c) Publicity for prizewinners — as part of ego boost.
(d) Catalogues might be geared to company's image.
(e) Experience of other organisations might be tapped.
(f) Could be introduced on a trial basis.
(g) As much risk as possible should be borne by the firm promoting the scheme.

CASE 10

The Welfare State

Cameos 1 to 3 — There are no "rights" and "wrongs" on these issues — just matters of opinion.
Examples of succour for "lame dogs":
National Government: Unemployment benefit
Local Authorities: Homes for Children deprived of parental care
Charitable bodies: The Samaritans coping with people who feel suicidal

CASE 11

The Good Shepherd — Second Assignment — Allocation of onerous duties.

	Options	Pros	Cons
(i)	To younger staff	A sort of apprenticeship?	Discouraging?
(ii)	To less industrious staff	Encourages them to leave or improve	Jobs badly done Danger of favouritism?
(iii)	In rotation	Spreads the burden Cover for sickness and holidays facilitated	Has to be organised

CASE 12

The Lame Dog

To support Fortescue's case

(i) Fortescue is one of the company's human assets. They have already staked substantial sums in him.

(ii) He might make a full recovery and be able to play a useful role again. His gratitude would encourage him to contribute in the future.

(iii) His experience could be useful even if he were employed in a less stressful role (with reduced pay?). He might be used in an advisory capacity — or in a training role.

(iv) Other staff who are being asked to extend themselves "to the limits" will be watching with interest what happens to a colleague who has "given his all".

(v) Would the loss of his job create stress? What effect would his death have on the staff?

"This is not a philanthropic institution"

(i) Fortescue is one man — the good of all the workforce must be considered. Profitability is essential if jobs are to survive.

(ii) The payments might set a precedent which has to be followed on all future occasions.

(iii) There is a duty to shareholders as well as to the workforce.

(iv) "Passengers" have to be carried — by their colleagues — some of whom are also overworked.

(v) It is for his own good. Work could create more stress.

CASE 13

Animal Experiments: Case Study

Among the arguments to use?

1. Akin to normal medical research. For example, how do you discover whether a new additive to canned food is carcinogenic?
2. What is the effect of inadequate testing? The Thalidomide babies — with the resultant claims on the manufacturers?
3. Many animals have short gestation periods. It is therefore easier to study genetic effects — reproduction etc.
4. Animals are generally expendable — and cheap. Rats do not invoke public sympathy.
5. Small animals require little space, food, attention and care.
6. Large numbers of experiments can be carried out.

CASE 14

The Distortion Barriers:
An Exercise in Communication

Pidgeon Savage and Lewis Inc., an American firm of consultants analysed the communication flow in 100 different American companies and found there was a loss of 30% of a communication at each level of management. What was the loss in your experiment?

CASE 15

A Free Press: Case Study

Some thoughts on the problems confronting Jeremy Wright:

1. Our disclosures might have saved a claim for damages if any injuries had occurred?
   We have sustained an interest in the product by continuing a discussion?
   If retraction is warranted it might be on the lines of:

   "In an article by. . . . in our (date) issue, attention was drawn to the possibility of an accident if certain procedures were not followed. This was in no way intended to imply. . . ."

The advertiser's compliance would be necessary if the object of the exercise was to be achieved.

On the other hand the newspaper has a social responsibility.

2. Find out what is being offered before we decide what action to take?
3. Ask the sub-editor to print a letter from Mr. Ogden — this latest letter perhaps?

CASE 16

Fresh Pastures

The Yellow Pages in the Telephone Directory will serve two purposes:

(i) They will help to give you ideas on the sort of businesses which are in existence, and
(ii) They will indicate the extent of the competition which might be expected in a particular type of business.

Local newspapers and the Thomson local directory might also help.
Ideas proposed might include:
A long-distance taxi-service (for the elderly?).
A mobile snack bar (for sports functions etc.).
An equipment hire shop (with ladders, electric saws etc.).

CASE 17

The Ice Age Cometh

If anyone in the group has artistic talents they can be demonstrated here. In evaluating the offerings two questions need to be borne in mind. First, "Which group of people are likely to be interested in the product?". Second, "Will the advertisement make an appropriate impact on this group?" In other words, good advertising is effective advertising.

CASE 18

A Shadow of the Truth

Study the geographic location of Agadir. Note its proximity to Madeira, the Canary Islands and Marrakesh. Consider its equable climate. What sort of holiday packages does this conjure up?

Decisions Required (inter alia)

Who is the holiday to be aimed at? It could be marketed outside the U.K.?

		Pros		*Cons*
A. Families	(i)	multiple bookings	(i)	limited to school holidays
			(ii)	childminders required
B. Students	(i)	would settle for basics	(i)	short of money
	(ii)	contacted through college magazines	(ii)	unruly behaviour
C. Retired	(i)	long season	(i)	need for medical attention
	(ii)	growth market	(ii)	too novel for this age group

How should we advertise? Who is to bear the cost?

A. Television	reaches a wide market	high cost per unit
B. Existing brochures	little expense	limited reach
C. Informal publicity	little or no expense	lack of certainty in the timing

Other decisions would need to be made about staffing and cuisine.

CASE 19

"As Madame wishes. . . ."

Recommendations could include:

  (i) Consulting with staff — an extended command meeting — individual interviews — or circulating a questionnaire — listening to their ideas — and any objections which emerge.

 (ii) Undertaking market research — consulting past and present customers — but how do we get reactions from potential customers:

(iii) Finding out whether any other organisations in the International Fashion Houses Group have coped with this problem.

(iv) Giving the late opening scheme a trial run of, say, three months.

 (v) Sending observer(s) from Head Office to study the situation first hand.

(vi) Examining workroom wages and conditions.

What sort of objections would you expect staff to raise? What alternatives can be suggested apart from the late opening scheme?

CASE 20

Hygiene on the Agenda

Item 1 — the immediate problem

Find out facts — send representative to Health Inspector — a senior member of staff. Which one?
The long term problem:
How to avoid future complaints? Redesign the work flow — double clean bottles — or use disposable bottles?

Item 2

Market research? Free samples? Through existing outlets? Disco theques? Feedback? An advertising campaign? Which media?

Item 3

Connection with Item 1? Find out facts. A senior member of staff to visit the Catering Manager? Which one? What can we do to win them back?

Item 4

Only male inspectors? Female part-timers? Longer breaks? Job rotation? Job enrichment? Consult existing staff? Exit interviews? Improved environment?

See Model Letter on p.195 indicating the sort of letter which might be written to deal with a complaint.

CASE 21

Limited Liability

Forming a company is simple and comparatively inexpensive. Your liability is limited to the amount invested through the purchase of the shares. Without this advantage, the whole of your personal estate could be used to pay off the business creditors, including your house, your car, and your personal possessions.

Disadvantages? Annual returns to the Registrar of Companies and the possibility that the profits of the company will be taxed at a higher rate (corporation tax) than those of an individual (income tax).

BELGARDA

Belgarda Limited, New Road, Carlton, Surrey CA17 4KY Tel 004 85600

Mrs. J. O'Connor,   30 April 198–.
368, Jordan Street,
Linton,   KJM/JSB
Surrey.

Dear Mrs O'Connor,

We were most concerned to learn, from the Manager of our Linton branch, that you believed your purchase of Belgarda Tuna may have been responsible for your daughter's being unwell. This product is obtained from a very reputable supplier whose standards generally are of the highest order. We were therefore extremely disturbed at this possibility.

Regrettably, as the sample you kindly returned had been opened for some time and in transit, conclusive microbiological tests could not be carried out to establish its condition at point of sale. Regrettably, also, we were unable to obtain a sample of the same code for examination as all had been sold. However, random control tests have been entirely satisfactory and no similar complaints have been received.

We can assure you that tuna fish for Belgarda is carefully selected and is prepared under conditions of stringent hygiene to our own high specifications. It is subjected to rigorous quality control at source and our own Food Chemists make regular checks on deliveries.

Our Canned Goods Buyer has explained that in cold weather the oil in the can may tend to thicken, but this does not detract from the product in any way and should not cause stomach upset. Our Chief Chemist added that sickness can result from numerous causes. Therefore, to establish its origins conclusively, it would be necessary to test samples of everything eaten and drunk by the sufferer for at least 48 hours prior to an attack.

We very much regret, therefore, that we are unable to present you with definite conclusions in this unfortunate matter. We are extremely sorry for the inconvenience and discomfort your daughter experienced but, in the light of the above, we think it possible that something other than the tuna caused her to be unwell. However, as there is no proof either way and as you were dissatisfied with your purchase, we would like to offer you the enclosed voucher for £2.50 as a gesture of goodwill and without prejudice.

Thank you for having taken the trouble to bring this matter to our attention.

Yours sincerely

Julia Bonner

Julia Bonner (Mrs)
Personal Assistant to Sales Director

CASE 22

Fair Shares for All

Advantages	*Disadvantages*
1. Contributions from Divisional Buyers, Finance & Photography.	1. Compromises are likely. Aim should be an "optimally effective catalogue" and not a "fair division".
2. The members as proposed expect to be consulted and would be aggrieved if they were ignored.	2. Time wasting. The members might have to listen, say, to Max Anning describing some of his special techniques — in detail.
3. Ideas can be exchanged. When Max Anning and Vincent Mancini explain their ideas, others may be swayed.	3. The committee members may not have equal stakes, though they have equal voting powers. Thus, 90% of the sales of Textiles and Furniture may be through Mail Order while only 10% of Clothing and Footwear are sold this way.
4. Understanding can be improved. "My problem is. . . ." Adrian Frisby can give the "global" view.	4. Cliques may develop such as Frisby's nominees versus Mancini's.

5. There will be fewer mistakes.	5. Some members of the committee may wield undue influence. e.g. "My father says. . . ." or "I agree with Vincent. . . ."

Problems for the committee to solve:
  (i) One person to be responsible overall? How much power is to be delegated?
  (ii) Who is to be in charge of the Package Holidays? And what about customer feedback?

CASE 23

Fleet Street — Next Stop

Points to be included in the memorandum?

For	*Against*
(a) Might cater for workers' social needs.	(a) Small circulation would lead to high cost per magazine.
(b) Staff might assume responsibility for production.	(b) Workforce is constantly changing.
(c) Advertising revenue?	(c) If workers were charged for the magazine they might be resentful.
(d) Could contribute to communication within company.	(d) If magazine is free it will not be valued.
(e) Could aid recruitment	(e) A monthly newsheet would be cheaper and more appropriate?

Other Thoughts?

Set up a committee? Give it a trial run? Find out what the workers think about the idea? Why foist it on them if they do not think it is a good idea?

CASE 24

Staff Opinion Poll (Part One)

Questions such as:

"What do you think of the firm's canteen facilities?"
A. Very good ☐ B. Good ☐ C. Average ☐ D. Bad ☐ E. Very bad ☐

Note extreme responses (A and E) and the neutral response at C.

CASE 25

Staff Opinion Poll (Part Two)

Among the questions to be answered:

1. Should staff sign the questionnaires?
   Easier to monitor — but staff may be inhibited.
2. Should the sample be stratified?
   Every section of staff covered — allows comparisons over time and between departments — but is more complex to administer.
3. What is the value of such a survey?
   It pinpoints problem areas — shows an interest in staff views and is cathartic when space is left for general comment. But it is expensive to set up and analyse. It also assumes that personnel staff with particular skills are available.
4. What is the value of an Index of Morale?
   It is an additional statistical measurement of managerial performance. However, alternatives such as rate of absenteeism and labour turnover are easier to calculate.

CASE 26

Pandora's Box

Who should hear about the allocation of the prize-money? The prize-winners. A letter from the Chief Executive preferably. The staff generally. Notice-boards. The staff magazine — photos if possible.

The public at large — for public relations. Local newspaper(s). How should the money be allocated? There is no obvious solution. It is simply an exercise in interaction.

CASE 27

"Friends, Romans, Countrymen . . ."

Options for Sales Manager (Exports):

		Pros	*Cons*
A.	Conference is inadvisable	cost saving	staff resentment
B.	Conference to be left as it stands	supports Davidson	negative?
C.	Advisable but changes called for such as. . . .	analytic	critical of colleague
D.	Advisable but drastic changes called for viz. . . .	positive	very critical of colleague

Related Options

   (i) Do *not* inform Davidson of developments.
  (ii) Inform Davidson *after* report has crystallised.
 (iii) Consult and confer *as* report crystallises.

Or along similar lines:
(a) discredit Davidson
(b) support him:
(c) be objective.

Bear in mind that Davidson could become your boss in 18 month's time.

Contributions to Discussion/Inclusions in Report

1. Representation from non-Sales staff.
2. Hold conference close to northern factories — include tour of factories in programme.
3. Reductions in cost? Cheaper hotels? Fewer representatives? Local conferences? Senior managers on tour?
4. For future reference get a feedback from participants.

CASE 28

Silence is Golden?

An abbreviated report follows such as might have been submitted to Brian Blakeney on his return. It should be easily seen to whom the report is addressed and from whom it has come. The date and the topic of the report are also vital pieces of information. The style of the report will vary according to individual tastes but it should always be borne in mind that a senior executive is likely to be a very busy person for whom time is at a premium. Subheadings will usually help the reader to digest the contents more effectively.

To Brian Blakeney Esq.,   From Carol Wood,
Managing Director.   Personnel Officer.
                                           15th April 1983

*Suggestions for Improving
Communications within the Works*

Following your instructions at the staff meeting on 3rd April, a number of discussions have taken place between Personnel staff in an attempt to find ways in which communications might be improved. With the Personnel Manager's approval, I am sending you this brief report setting out our conclusions.

1. *Joint Consultation*

While it is usual for the existing Joint Consultation committee to meet from time to time to deal with problems needing urgent attention, there would be merit in arranging for regular meetings to take place. We appreciate that this would involve the Shop Stewards spending more time away from their work, but regular access to Senior Managers provide certain benefits. For example:

(a) Managers would receive early warning of problems affecting industrial relations.
(b) Grievances could receive early and authoritative attention.
(c) Managers could use the meetings to put over their views and explain their difficulties and their plans.
(d) A mutually acceptable degree of socialisation should take place with the objective of breaking down the barriers between "them" and "us". In a highly competitive world such as ours, we stand to succeed or fail as a team.

Crisis meetings could still be held as and when required, but hopefully regular meetings such as are proposed would reduce the number of crises we have to face anyway.

2. *Induction Procedures*

When employees first join the company, they usually start with at least a modicum of enthusiasm. They are shown round the works rather briefly and thereafter largely ignored. It would be surprising if their early enthusiasm was not substantially eroded.

What is suggested is that newcomers would benefit from meeting the managers and hearing from them personally about the history of the company and our plans for the future. Although the additional burden on the Senior Managers is recognised, it is felt that contacts such as these would prove invaluable in the long run.

3. *Management Contact with the Workforce*

Many of the old hands at Destry often say they see less of the Senior Managers than they did in the "old days". This is partly the result of the growth in the size of the firm and the complexities of the new methods of marketing and production. However, it seems that the workers appreciate these personal contacts. If managers are aware of this, they will no doubt take the necessary steps to generate the sort of favourable atmosphere which will reflect in higher levels of production and more harmonious industrial relations.

In Conclusion

I trust these suggestions are helpful and no doubt you will let me know if there is anything further required of me. I would be happy to clarify or elaborate any or all of the above suggestions.

Carol Wood

CASE 29

Reassurance Needed

The basic tenet? The larger the organisation becomes, the lower the morale. The reason? As communications pass through the various managerial levels they become distorted. In the case of Cromwell Insurance this has produced:

(i) a flood of clerical errors;

(ii) liquidity problems (managerial miscalculations).

Immediate Problem — Liquidity

A. Negotiate loans with bankers — offering shares or buildings as security.

B. Liquidate some existing assets such as stocks and shares — insurance companies usually hold medium-dated government stocks.

C. Avoid distribution of profits and dividends — these would deplete the cash available.

D. Consider making a new issue of shares to existing shareholders — called rights issues.

E. Raise the premiums on the insurance policies.

F. Jettison the U.S. connections.

G. Reconsider the range of insurance policies offered. Which are unprofitable? Jettison the unprofitable business.

Clerical Errors

A. Decentralisation — setting up subsidiaries — different departments.

B. Job enrichment.

C. Staff attitude survey.

D. Overtime paid to selected staff while they clear the backlog.

E. Consult staff/Supervisors/Personnel Department/Chief Inspector.

CASE 30

Absenteeism and Lateness

Alison Page — The Manager should interview her first and explain the problems which are emerging. Ask her how she thinks the problems can be solved? If this does not bring about improvements:

(a) allocate the less pleasant jobs to her,

(b) withhold increments where salary scales are in force,

(c) ask Personnel Department to issue a warning as part of the process of dismissal, or

(d) where the contract of employment allows, recommend transfer to another branch.

Richard Meacher — The Manager should interview him about his problems generally. Specifically:

(a) encourage him to make a break from his home environment,
(b) recommend transfer to another branch as a way of enforcing this,
(c) withhold increments (or threaten to do so), and
(d) as a matter of urgency, discuss appearance and his responses on the telephone. It must be emphasised that customers/clients are often only able to judge the efficiency and attitude of the Company through their telephone conversations with staff.

CASE 31

Top of the Pops

A good timekeeping/attendance allowance might be introduced, by means of which those who miss work or arrive late on any one day lose the bonus otherwise available. The scheme could be introduced when a new level of pay is negotiated. "We agree to pay an extra £6 a week, but £3 will only be payable for those who come to work — on time!" Music at work might be introduced to reduce the tedium (see Compendium). Similarly, the total working environment might be examined (see under Ergonomics in Compendium).

CASE 32

Refer back to Fig. 3. on page 13.

CASE 33

No obvious choice, but an exercise in interaction.

CASE 34

Limited Progress

Should poor performance in low grade posts affect selection for higher grade posts?

(i) How else can staff prove their ability/determination?
(ii) Different and even opposite qualities are called for — such as a "questionning approach"?
(iii) What factors should be considered when promotion is being considered? Loyalty? Past performance? Breadth of experience? Ability to do the work? Acceptability?

Is "unacceptability" Jim's problem in Gellan Products? If interviewing "prejudiced" candidates is a problem, how do you think the problem should be tackled?:

Options?

   A. Keep Jim 'out of sight' — on less contentious jobs?
   B. Get the prejudiced candidates used to the idea that they
      live in a *multi-racial society*? Does everyone in society
      have a duty to ensure that minorities are not oppressed?

   Note that the Race Relations Act 1976 prohibits
   discrimination on racial grounds.

   How should Reg react to John's advice?;

   A. Cross Jim off the list — "It's not my problem?"
   B. See Jim for himself and make his own judgement? Does
      he advise John of his plans?

CASE 35

Role Playing: Case Study

Merits

   (i) Boardroom skills can be acquired by the potential
       Directors.
   (ii) Issues could be discussed before/after they are put to the
        Senior Board (their contributions could be valuable).
   (iii) Could reduce the workload for the main Board.
   (iv) Would allow individuals to be assessed before they are
        promoted to the Senior Board.
   (v) provides motivation and recognition to meritorious
       executives.
   (iv) Allows one of the senior Directors to function on the
        Shadow Board to see how the "candidates" get on with
        each other.

Demerits?

   (i) Costs — allocation of room — and secretariat — executive's time
   (ii) Possible jealousies, and what about those who are rejected?
   (iii) Degree of overlapping is wasteful, and where does responsibility for
         errors lie?

CASE 36

Our Daily Bread

No obvious choice. An exercise in interaction.

CASE 37

Sixth Time Lucky

Advice?

A. A "glowing" job description will produce many applications. The costs involved would include:
   (i) vetting of applications,
   (ii) correspondence,
   (iii) interviews.
B. A "down-to-earth" job description will produce too few candidates — many of the best staff will be deterred from applying.

Basic problem?

Qualified chemist required for a routine job — "he doesn't mention money" — he was presumably attracted by the money in the first place — but his enthusiasm was quickly eroded once he became aware of the routine nature of the work.

Options?

1. Accept the situation and the need to incur the costs of labour turnover.
2. Try to find someone who is suitable *and* likely to stay e.g. a married woman with family commitments.
3. Redesign the job by introducing;
   (i) an unqualified assistant to take over the routine work;
   (ii) additional responsibilities such as dealing with consumer complaints or assuming control of some line operations.

Draft advertisement

1. Give a profile of the ideal candidate — "The ideal person we are looking for. . . ."

2. Indicate the nature of the work — "The work essentially involves. . . ."
3. Indicate the attractive aspects of the environment.

CASE 38

The Wide Open Spaces

Recommendations:

(a) Use own girls for t.v. advertising.
(b) Job enrichment/rotation.
(c) Increase the range of products — diversify.
(d) Offer a bonus for good timekeeping/attendance.
(e) Find out what the problems are by consulting.:
   (i) line workers;
   (ii) line managers;
   (iii) personnel department;
   (iv) staff leaving (exit interviews).
(f) Employ more part-time female workers.
(g) Publicise prosecutions for pilfering, and/or
(h) Offer workers unlimited (?) quantities at 'cost'.
(i) Examine complaints from customers to find out what is going wrong.
(j) Créches for young mothers.
(k) Shorter working hours coupled with shift work.
(l) Flexible working hours.
(m) Changes in the pattern of breaks.
(n) Music while they work.
(o) Suggestion schemes with prizes.
(p) Introduction of production targets at every level.

CASE 39

Leadership: Case Study

John Young — enthusiastic — capable — one of the company's
               human assets — but likely to be eroded?
Joe Brent   — also a human asset — but prejudging his new P.A.?

Required

A change of attitude by Brent? Through an informal discussion with Dan

Davis? A working lunch — discussing many things? Encourage self-criticism — emphasise cost of labour turnover? Need for supportive management?:

Supportive Management

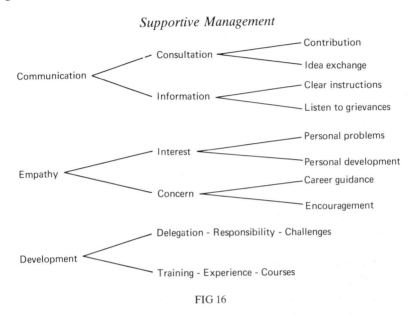

FIG 16

CASE 40

The Whiz Kid

Evaluation of proposals:

(a) Effect of changes on staff morale? Have staff and/or customers been consulted? Is the new General Manager aware of the likely effects?

(b) Danger of a vicious circle? Fewer customers — loss of job satisfaction for staff — falling revenue — necessitating further cuts.

(c) Effects of new policy may be delayed and therefore camouflaged. Clients are committed to this year's holidays.

(d) A deliberate switch into a down-market segment could be beneficial. Has any market research been carried out?

(e) How would students be recruited?

(f) Why not introduce changes on a trial basis? Or introduce "economy class" on a small scale and study results?

(g) Profit maximising and cost minimising is laudable but company's excellent reputation can be dissipated in return for immediate profits.

CASE 41

Unit Five

Options?:

A. Offer him more pay or promotion — he may be seeking status.
B. Offer him some shares in the company — perhaps an Executive Share Option — or a Directorship.
C. Interview him at length — a formal lunch with Morris? What is he looking for? What are his plans?
D. Accept his departure but show gratitude for his past efforts?:

   (i) Delay his departure as long as possible?
  (ii) Protect the company as regards patents etc.?
 (iii) Review existing members of staff to consider possible substitutes for Danny?
 (iv) Advertise for a new designer?

E. Offer to finance his new venture — assuming it looks O.K.?

   (i) Set up a subsidiary — on a larger scale than he anticipates,
  (ii) Use the whole or part of the Bristol factory development.
 (iii) Keep majority of voting shares in the new company in the name of either Morris Steiner or Gamma Ltd.
 (iv) Use Danny's name in the title of the company — e.g. Danny Schaffer Productions Ltd. — ego food.
  (v) If the venture is risky, Gamma should take Secured Debentures instead of equities.

For Future Reference

Ensure that no person in the organisation is indispensable. Anticipate this sort of situation and develop strategies to cope. Examine staff training and development programmes and plan for long-term succession to key posts.

CASE 42

An Immovable Object

Summary of problem:

On the evidence available, the Liverpool plant is more profitable than Oxford. The possible explanation is that Management by Objectives and Job Enrichment produce the better results for Chris Amber at Liverpool. But there are no past figures. These techniques need to be introduced at

Oxford — against the resistance of Charles Bertwell, an influential share-holder and the Managing Director.

Options available	Pros	Cons
(a) Show Bertwell the statistics and hope he takes notice	confrontation avoided	he may not respond
(b) Show him the statistics and ask him how he accounts for the differences	he would be forced to justify his policies	he may offer other explanations
(c) A direct approach viz. "We think MBO and JE pay off. Here's the evidence!".	unambiguous and straightforward	might force him into a confrontation
(d) Discuss his succession with him — he is 59. Try to influence his choice of heir	an eventual change of policy	he may select a traditionalist as his heir
(e) Interchange senior staff 'to improve efficiency'	a chance to influence the Bertwell executives	the idea could backfire
(f) Offer Bertwell a post on the board of the holding company	he would give up control of Bertwells	he may still retain the control of Bertwells

CASE 43

Them v. Us: Case Study

Some contributions to the discussion:

1. Management may be hard put to justify the dismissal if what Duffy says is true. In similar circumstances (Ayab v. Vauxhall Motors Ltd. 1978) an Industrial Tribunal found a dismissal was unfair because one worker had been treated differently from others on the same shift.
2. Full searches are bound to case resentment among innocent parties, yet in this firm the interests of the workers suffer as a result of the pilfering. A few prosecutions or dismissals — after adequate warnings — might avoid the need for further searches — at least on such a scale.
3. It is only by 'co-operating' that the committee can find out what is going on? There is scope for productivity bargaining here. Conces-

sions can be used as bargaining counters by both sides.
"We will agree to *this* — if you agree to . . . . ."

4. Excessive wage claims can have the effect of reducing profits and raising prices to the detriment of sales. Moderation in the next round of pay talks might be necessary?

5. What has happened to change Management's mind on this issue?

CASE 44

In the Moonlight

Refer to Compendium for an explanation of dismissal procedures.

CASE 45

If You Can't Beat Them — Join Them!

For	Against
1. A formal gesture — but motives need to be explained.	1. What would a worker know about boardroom policies & procedures?
2. The worker would be outvoted continually?	2. For how long could a worker carry the support of his mates?
3. His contributions would be useful.	3. Would he not be ostracised in effect by the other Directors? Director's lunches for example?
4. He could be used as an extra line of communication.	4. How would he be dealt with when workers' wage claims were being discussed by the Board?
5. He might be won over and become an ally?	5. How would he be paid for his boardroom duties? And would he be expected to acquire a minimum shareholding like the other Directors?
6. Since more worker participation is likely in the future (consider the E.E.C.), the company should be gaining experience.	6. Would workers see this as a sign of weakness and demand more?

Other Comments

How would appointee be selected? What would happen if he was deliberately and/or consistently obstructive in the boardroom? What are the alternatives to worker directors?

CASE 46

The Magna Carta

Options?
   A. Involve workforce *ab initio*.
   B. Managers to prepare constitution and present it as a *fait accompli*.
   C. Managers determine basic framework, leaving workers to deal with remainder.

Number of representatives/A grid for representation? Total workforce = 1034, so if there are 50 workers to each representative the Council will consist of approximately 21 workers plus the management representatives. 21 votes to 3?

Divided by Categories?

In this case the 79 foremen would elect one representative — as would the supervisors. But all the other representatives could come from the assembly lines.

Divided by Departments?

This would give 13 representatives to assembly lines — one representative for the office etc. But no foremen or supervisors are likely to be appointed.

Leave the Workers to Decide the Make-up of the Council?

Matters covered should include:

   (i) Voting procedures — including requirements for changes to constitution.
  (ii) Set up grievance procedures but exclude wage negotiations.
 (iii) Formulate a disciplinary code — with workers' support.
  (iv) Set up consultation procedures for innovations etc.
   (v) Car parking arrangements — holiday rotas — social activities — canteen facilities etc.

Note: The Works Manager should try to find out the experiences of other companies which have trod this path.

CASE 47

Double or Quits

Reasons for Resistance

(a) *Economic factors*

    (i) Fears for economic welfare — redundancy linked with auto mation — microprocessors etc.

    (ii) Remuneration — new systems of job evaluation — amendments to wages/salaries — changes in differentials.

(b) *Resentment to new orders and/or increased control*

    (i) Any change must increase the number of orders managers give to subordinates.

    (ii) Many changes are initiated by staff officers while line managers are confronted with the problems of implementation.

    (iii) Organisational changes will involve changes of status and new lines of communication. New relationships will need to be established.

(c) *Inconvenience*

    (i) A worker is likely to object to the assignment of extra duties — initially at least.

    (ii) Learning new procedures requires the expenditure of energy and human beings tend to be lazy.

(d) *Uncertainty*

    (i) The worker knows what his present circumstances are. He does not know what the new ones will be. Uncertainty is always a threat.

    (ii) When there is change a communications vacuum is likely to be filled by rumour and speculation.

(e) *Threats to interpersonal relationships*

    (i) People do not like the disruption of existing relationships and the work involved in establishing new ones.

    (ii) Changing work patterns upset existing and accepted patterns of co-operation and leadership.

(f) *Union attitudes*

    (i) The Unions are representing their members who will generally expect them to oppose Management.

    (ii) Since they represent many workers, the resistance will be organised and therefore more effective.

Overcoming Resistance to Change

1. Financial incentives may be offered where the resistance is based on

economic factors.

2. Economic fears may be removed by guaranteeing that no-one will suffer a loss of job or loss of earnings. This is an expensive remedy, particularly as the change is likely to be aimed at reducing (labour) costs. However, the workforce may be run down through "natural wastage".

3. Exerting supervisory pressure may be possible, particularly when there is a scarcity of jobs generally.

4. Changes may be introduced tentatively — on a trial basis.

5. Management might encourage small scale changes all the time so that change becomes the norm — and is acceptable.

6. Two-way communication can be improved.

7. The group can be allowed to participate in the decision-making process (see pages 22/3)

8. Obtaining Union approval may be a pre-requisite to change. Bargaining may be necessary. For example, "We are prepared to guarantee there will be no redundancies, if you are prepared to accept the employment of women on the new equipment."

Note

The technique is to find out why there is resistance — or why there is likely to be resistance — and then apply an appropriate remedy. In the same way, a doctor diagnoses a sickness and then prescribes the medicine to combat the particular disease.

CASE 48

The Residuary Legatee

Bearing in mind that substantial death duties (called Capital Transfer Tax) will need to be raised — presumably from the sale of shares being transferred to Alan Bull, two different problems confront him.

Short Term Problems

A. Find out from the Company Secretary/Board of Directors whether plans are afoot to find a replacement for the Chief Executive.

B. Instruct the Managing Director to:
   (i) Order the machine guards forthwith.
   (ii) Accept the shop steward's claims at this point of time to avoid industrial action.
   (iii) Seek a moratorium until a new Managing Director is appointed.
   (iv) Resist all claims.

Long Term Problems

A. Find a purchase for the shares as soon as possible — are the shares quoted on a Stock Exchange?
B. Pay the death duties out of his own funds — or get a bank loan so that he can do so — in this way he can retain a controlling interest.
C. Find a company which is prepared to take over J. Bull Ltd.
D. Seek the aid of an institution like the Estate Duty Investment Trust which specialises in providing this type of finance.
E. Appoint a new Managing Director:
(i) From within the Company.
(ii) After advertising — through a specialist agency.
F. Try to persuade the present Managing Director to stay
G. Take over the role of Chief Executive himself.

CASE 49

Milking Time

Recommendations:

1. Ask insurance company what measures would be required to make the risk insurable again (Could an insurance "pool" be set up within the group of companies?)
2. Consult the unions to find out their specific grievances.
3. Consult line managers.
4. Organise a safety campaign in conjunction with Unions.
(i) safety committees:
(ii) research;
(iii) records;
(iv) safety training;
(v) poster campaign;
(vi) equipment;
(vii) board appointment of Safety Officer.
5. Redesign jobs — reduce boredom — responsibility.
6. Experience within the Group? Send party from London? Invite Melhuish to London?
7. Offer a no-accident bonus scheme to all foundry workers?
(i) Individual basis?
(ii) Group basis?
8. Long lines of control. Need for decentralisation.
9. Generous treatment to next of kin — beyond legal requirement — to demonstrate company's concern.
10. Attempt to produce a spirit of co-operation with Unions — co-existence v. confrontation — listen — through Works Councils — participation etc.

CASE 50

Lies, Damned Lies!

There is a danger here of the Managing Director being lured into a rebuttal of the claims made about his personal finances. He obviously does earn more than the shop floor workers. Why bother to argue about that? He would be better advised to find out exactly who the Workers Action Committee represent. Are they representing workers at Hayford and Mannering — if so what about the Unions — and the shop stewards?

CASE 51

The Fairest in the land

Among the notions generated might be the following:
1. Unions are crisis-orientated. Moderates stay away from meetings until there is a crisis. By then, militants/extremists might have taken over.
2. Unions have communication problems like other organisations. The leadership is therefore sometimes under a misapprehension about rank and file feeling — and vice versa.
3. One employer might have to face a number of different unions. And the unions are often in conflict with each other — leading to demarcation disputes.

CASE 52

Heads and Tails

Ideas such as the following might be put forward:
1. The individual company attempts to produce a rational pay structure within the organisation by Job Evaluation. Why is no attempt made to apply this concept nationally?
2. Co-ownership schemes. Favourable tax concessions such as those introduced in the Finance Act 1980 encourage companies to issue voting shares to workers — thereby reducing the gap between "them" and "us".
3. Participation in the decision-making process — worker directors (see Case No. 45) — Works Councils (see Case No. 46) — two-tier Boards of Directors (as in Germany) with 50% worker representation on the Supervisory Board?

Index

A compendium of terms is shown separately on pages 161–80.

217